STEAM Projects

Observation, Experimentation, & Presentation

Author: Linda Armstrong
Editor: Mary Dieterich
Proofreaders: Margaret Brown and April Albert

COPYRIGHT © 2019 Mark Twain Media, Inc.

ISBN 978-1-62223-766-1

Printing No. CD-405032

Mark Twain Media, Inc., Publishers
Distributed by Carson-Dellosa Publishing LLC

Table of Contents

Table of Contents (cont.)

Introduction

Science, technology, engineering, arts, and mathematics underlie every aspect of contemporary civilization, from the buildings that shelter us, to the food that nourishes us, the water that sustains us, the vehicles that transport us, the devices that connect us, and the platforms that send our imaginations soaring.

The projects and resources in *STEAM Projects* will help middle-school students see connections among these vital fields and provide opportunities to engage with them. The key here is engagement. Rather than reading about a scientific or technological process, then answering questions, students will experiment, observe phenomena, and present research findings. If demonstrations are called for, students, not instructors, will perform and explain them.

This text is not meant to be comprehensive. As an overview, it offers a quick taste of science disciplines covered at this level. Use these projects, not to replace, but to spice up your regular program.

Features of This Book and Its Pages

This book's projects are brief. Students should be able to complete most in a single session or less. Those who wish to study a subject in depth will find extensions and resources on each page. Because students will perform any experiments or demonstrations, this book's projects emphasize safe, convenient materials and technology.

The text includes links to important, dramatic, or interesting demonstrations online. Teachers may view and recreate some of them in class, if desired.

Each page lists suggested materials at the top. The student procedure takes students through the steps in the project. Extensions are listed for further student exploration and experimentation. At the bottom, a reference box includes:

- Science fair suggestions
- Resources for teachers
- Covered STEAM skills

The arts and sciences are naturally exciting. They stimulate curiosity and creativity. Using them together in hands-on projects like the ones suggested in this book could ignite lifelong passions in your students.

Swinging Masterpieces: Pendulum Painting

Objective: To investigate the behavior of a pendulum and explore the possibilities of random line artwork.

Materials:

Plastic dispenser bottle (for ketchup, mustard, or glue)   Large sheet of white paper
Liquid tempera paint (thinned so it will flow out of the bottle's tip)
Tripod (Use a photo tripod, find online directions, or provide materials and challenge students
    to design a stable tripod in a separate session.)
Scissors   Hole punch   3 pieces of string (at least a meter long)

Student Procedure:

- Cut the bottom off the bottle. Poke three holes at equal distances around its exposed base. Attach one end of a string through each hole.
- Hold the three long loose ends together at the top. Attach them to the underside of the tripod to create a pendulum bob. The bottle will hang with the dispenser point facing down.
- Place the paper under the tripod.
- Fill the container with a small amount of tempera to start. (Make sure it is thin enough to come out of the tip without squeezing.)
- Record a prediction of the number of swings before the bob hangs still.
- Lift the bob and release. Record the results.
- Share how Newton's Laws of Motion apply to this pendulum. Explain why clocks, before electricity, used pendulums.

Extensions:

- Research the history of the pendulum. Present it on a webpage.
- Explain how a special pendulum can demonstrate the rotation of the earth.
- Predict how a pendulum might behave on the surface of another specific planet or moon in our solar system.
- Learn and perform the song "My Grandfather's Clock" or another piece of music based on the sound of a clock. Create a musical instrument to simulate the ticking.
- What kind of pendulum do musicians use when practicing? How is it different from this pendulum?
- Plan a display showing the inside of a pendulum clock with gears. Explain how energy from the pendulum moves the hands.

Resources for Teachers:

Physics Quanta: The Pendulum's Swing
    https://galileospendulum.org/2011/05/24/physics-quanta-the-pendulums-swing/
Swinging Pendulum (for High School)
    https://www.teachengineering.org/activities/view/cub_energy_lesson03_activity2

STEAM Skills:

Science: physics, Newton's Laws of Motion, pendulums
Technology: historic methods of telling time and their impact on society
Engineering: designing a tripod, analyzing or modeling the inside of a pendulum clock
Arts: pendulum tempera painting, musical performance, creating instruments
Mathematics: Advanced: using mathematical data to predict behavior of a pendulum on another planet, or explaining what mathematical processes would be used

The Great Book Drop: Predicting Gravity

Objective: To investigate the effect of gravity on objects with differing masses.

Materials:
Several books with similar dimensions but differing masses (some should be noticeably lighter)
Scale   Ruler

Student Procedure:
- Lift the books and explain how they are the same and how they are different.
- Use scales and rulers to quantify and record observations.
- Predict which will land first when any two books are dropped to the floor at the same time.
- Drop the books and record the results. Repeat the experiment with the same books.
- Try the experiment again with different pairs of books. Try dropping books shorter or longer distances.
- Measure and record the distances carefully.
- Present the results on a chart or graph, then compare the charts to those of other students.
- Research the famous origin of this experiment.
- Thespians write a skit depicting the event and act it out. Artists draw cartoons for a slide show or booklet.

Extensions:
- Try the same experiment with a small thick paperback novel and a large thin paperback children's picture book. Record and explain the result.
- Construct a simple balance. Find a fulcrum that allows a heavy object and a light one to balance. Quantify your results.
- Plan a display showing the weight of an average person your age on different planets.
- Explain how gravity can generate electricity.
- Plan a slide show demonstrating how the world's tides are driven by gravity. Explain why the moon's gravity affects the oceans more than the land.
- Draw the stages of a landslide or rockslide. Use arrows to show the pull of gravity.
- Make a video explaining Isaac Newton's association with an apple. Explain why narratives are important (and can be misleading) in science.

Resources for Teachers:
Terrestrial Gravity: Galileo Analyzes a Cannonball Trajectory
http://galileo.phys.virginia.edu/classes/152.mf1i.spring02/DiscoveringGravity.htm

STEAM Skills:
Science: physics, gravity, weight, electricity, tides, Isaac Newton
Technology: researching hydroelectric power generation, using measuring devices, video equipment, presentation software
Engineering: designing scales and using fulcrums
Arts: visually depicting a series of steps or events, recreating an event in a dramatic skit, evaluating the influence of narrative in science
Mathematics: measurement, graphs

The Mysterious Disappearing Color Spinner

Objective: To demonstrate that white light contains all colors.

Materials:

Plastic straw   Straight pin   Colored markers   Compass   Protractor
White cardboard disc 3" in diameter (can use a white paper plate)   Scissors
For Extensions: a glass prism or faceted glass crystal, tempera paints

Student Procedure:

- Use a pattern or a compass to draw a 3" diameter circle on a piece of white, lightweight cardboard (a paper plate will work).
- Cut it out, then use a protractor to divide it into seven (advanced) or six (easy) equal sections.
- Solidly fill each section with one of the following colors in this order: red, orange, yellow, green, blue, indigo, (and/or violet).
- Place the pin in the center of the disc and set the disc with the pin in the end of the straw.
- Record predictions of what will happen.
- Spin the disc as fast as possible. Observe and explain the result.

Extensions:

- Use tempera or watercolor to mix the same colors used above together. Explain your result.
- Interview the stage crew at school. Learn how colored lights are used in stage productions. When would this technology be useful?
- Try shining different colors of light through a glass prism or faceted glass crystal. What changes do you notice?

Resources for Teachers:

The Electromagnetic Spectrum: NASA
    https://rmpbs.pbslearningmedia.org/resource/phy03.sci.phys.energy.nasaspectrum/the-electromagnetic-spectrum-nasa/?#.W32R785KhaQ
Light Is Waves: Crash Course Physics #39 https://www.youtube.com/watch?v=IRBfpBPELmE
Newton Disc https://ipfs.io/ipfs/QmXoypizjW3WknFiJnKLwHCnL72vedxjQkDDP1mXWo6uco/wiki/Newton_disc.html
All Our Favorite Ways to Teach Color Theory in One Place!
    https://www.theartofed.com/2015/09/21/all-our-favorite-ways-to-teach-color-theory-in-one-place/
Stage Lighting FAQ https://www.theatrefolk.com/blog/awesome-stage-lighting-resource/

STEAM Skills:

Science: physics, waves, optics, light
Technology: researching stage lighting
Engineering: creating a spinner
Arts: the color wheel, color mixing. stage lighting
Mathematics: geometry, using a compass, using a protractor

Domino Tumble: The Transfer of Energy in a Mechanical Wave

Objective: To generate and observe the transfer of mechanical energy in a wave.

Materials:

Sets of dominoes   Flat horizontal surface
Optional: smartphone, tablet, laptop, or another video recording device

Student Procedure:

- Set the dominoes on end. Each piece should be close enough to the next to knock it down.
- When all the dominoes are set up, record predictions, and knock down a single domino on one end.
- Observe the wave travel the length of the setup.
- Write a brief explanation of observations, including the source of the energy transferred in the wave, as well as the roles of both gravity and Newton's First Law of Motion in the experiment.
- If desired, document the domino fall in a short video, along with an explanation of forces at work.

Extensions:

If Slinky™ toy springs are available, students will be able to experience the difference between transverse and longitudinal waves.

- Compressing the spring will create longitudinal waves (particles move in the same direction as the wave).
- Moving one end of the Slinky™ up and down will generate transverse waves (particles move perpendicular to the direction of the wave). Ocean breakers are transverse.

Resources for Teachers:

Wave Propagation: Ripples on a Pond
  https://www.iris.edu/hq/inclass/video/wave_propagation_ripples_on_a_pond
More About Transverse and Longitudinal Waves
  https://airandspace.si.edu/sites/default/files/media-assets/STEM%20in%2030_Using%20
  Waves%20to%20Communicate.pdf
A Domino Display
  https://www.youtube.com/watch?v=PsLHWqWg1N4

STEAM Skills:

Science: physics, waves, energy, Newton's First Law of Motion, gravity
Technology: using video equipment and software (optional)
Engineering: arranging the dominoes at the optimum distance
Arts: video, kinetic art
Mathematics: measuring the time it takes for the dominoes to fall

Canned Vibrations: Volume and Pitch

Objective: To observe the effects of container size and composition on the volume and pitch of sound.

Materials:

Containers of various sizes with lids that stay securely closed: cans, plastic drinking bottles, empty cardboard cartons, wooden boxes, plastic eggs, paper towel tubes
Noisemakers: beans, pebbles, BBs, rice, sand, dried corn, shells, buttons, dried peas, paper clips   Masking or duct tape   Labels
Smartphone, tablet, laptop, or another video/audio recording device

Student Procedure:

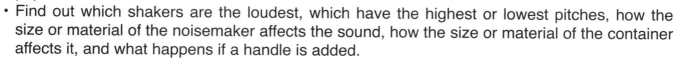

- Create percussion instruments (shakers) using a variety of containers.
- Use only one type of noisemaker inside each container. Label the container with the type of noisemaker inside.
- Tape the lids in place if they do not already stay closed or for the ends of paper towel tubes.
- Find out which shakers are the loudest, which have the highest or lowest pitches, how the size or material of the noisemaker affects the sound, how the size or material of the container affects it, and what happens if a handle is added.
- Working individually or as a group, create a percussion background for a song or rap verse using various shakers. Make a sound or video recording.

Extensions:

- Make a kazoo by folding waxed paper over a comb. Notice the vibrations as you hum notes at different pitches.
- Fill water bottles with different amounts of water. Blow over the top of each. Observe differences in pitch. Fill glasses with different amounts of water and strike each with a spoon. Play a tune.
- Use rubber bands and a box to create a stringed instrument.

Resources for Teachers:

Chrome Music Lab: Sound Waves
https://musiclab.chromeexperiments.com/Sound-Waves/
Fascinating Facts About Sound Waves
https://www.svconline.com/news/fascinating-facts-about-sound-waves-370442
Virtual Oscilloscope
https://academo.org/demos/virtual-oscilloscope/
Musical Instruments for Kids to Make
https://feltmagnet.com/crafts/Music-Instruments-for-Kids-to-Make

STEAM Skills:

Science: physics, sound waves, volume, pitch
Technology: using video/audio recording equipment, using an online oscilloscope
Engineering: studying the design of musical instruments
Arts: music, percussion
Mathematics: reading the graph on an oscilloscope, measuring water for bottles or glasses

Rough Roads: Toy Cars Meet Friction

Objective: To observe the effects of friction on a rolling object.

Materials:

Small metal toy cars   Stopwatch or digital timer
A four- or six-foot wood plank with cardboard guardrails on either side
Books to prop up one end of the plank
Aluminum foil   Smooth, rough, and very rough sandpaper sheets

Student Procedure:

- Prop up the prepared plank on one end to create a slanted track.
- Cover the plank with foil.
- Roll the car down the plank, and time it with a stopwatch or digital timer.
- Replace the foil with fine sandpaper sheets. Roll the car down. Does it roll faster or slower?
- Repeat with the rough and very rough sandpaper.
- Considering the result, why are roads textured instead of smooth? Why are wet streets more dangerous than dry pavement?
- Explain how your answers relate to Newton's First Law of Motion.
- Optional: Create or find a graph online to show supporting data such as stopping distances on wet and dry streets.

Extensions:

- Friction influences fuel economy. Find out what automotive engineers are doing to work with it. Could energy generated by friction be used to help power a car? Search to find out.
- Use friction to paint grass. Use tempera or acrylic paint, textured paper, and a flat brush. Dip the brush into green paint. Use a paper towel to squeeze out most of it. Spread the brush bristles apart. Use short upward motions on the paper to suggest grass blades. Experiment with wet and dry brushstrokes.
- See these scrapers (musical instruments) in the Metropolitan Museum of Art.
      https://www.metmuseum.org/art/collection/search/501286
  How do they depend on friction? Design one of your own.

Resources for Teachers:

Experimenting with Forces of Motion—The Force of Friction
   https://www.youtube.com/watch?v=Wg9QNZmlsDY
Friction Powerpoint Story Style
   https://www.tes.com/teaching-resource/friction-powerpoint-story-style-6331032
19 Fun Ideas & Resources for Force and Motion
   http://www.teachjunkie.com/sciences/19-fun-ideas-resources-force-and-motion/

STEAM Skills:

Science: physics, friction
Technology: researching road design, using a stopwatch or digital timer
Engineering: researching tire design
Arts: wet and dry brush painting, scrapers (music)
Mathematics: graphing, measuring time

Let There Be Light: Balloon Static Electricity

Objective: To investigate the properties of static electricity.

Materials:

Balloons   Low-wattage fluorescent light tubes
Copy paper   Colored pencils or markers

Student Procedure:

- Inflate and secure the opening of a balloon.
- Rub the balloon against your hair. Lift the balloon up. Observe what happens to your hair.
- Hold the charged balloon near a wall. Observe what happens.
- Tear a sheet of used copy paper into little pieces. Place them on a table. Hold the balloon over them. Observe what happens.
- Rub the balloon on something fuzzy like a sweater. Touch it to the end of the light tube.
- Use a text or the Internet to find out what causes static electricity. Design a poster showing what happens when the balloon acquires a negative charge.

Extensions:

- Use a smartphone or laptop to video the experiments on this page. Include your poster and explain what is happening.
- Lightning is static electricity on a large scale. Design a display showing how it forms and what people should do to stay safe.
- Research how lightning rods work. Design a poster to explain.
- Research Benjamin Franklin's experiments with electricity. Pretend you are Franklin. Present a short monologue about your experiences.

Science Fair Project Idea: Find out how fabric softeners prevent static. Compare several. Create a graph to show which works best.

Resources for Teachers:

Lightning: Static Electricity
   http://www.edu.pe.ca/gray/class_pages/krcutcliffe/physics521/21fields/articles/Lightning%20-%20Static%20Electricity.htm
Take Charge! All About Static Electricity
   https://www.teachengineering.org/lessons/view/cub_electricity_lesson02

STEAM Skills:

Science: physics, static electricity, lightning, electrons
Technology: using the Internet, lightning protection
Engineering: preventing static with fabric softeners, researching lightning rods
Arts: designing an informative poster, dramatic monologue
Mathematics: graphing

May the Best Bulb Win: Light vs Heat

Objective: To investigate the relationship between heat and light energy.

Materials: (save bulb packaging for wattage information)
    LED bulb 800 lumens   Incandescent bulb 800 lumens
    Halogen bulb 800 lumens   Compact Fluorescent bulb 800 lumens
    A desk lamp with socket for bulbs or separate desk lamps for each bulb
    Electrical outlet   Thermometer   Stopwatch or digital timer

Student Procedure:
- Place the thermometer on the table.
- Screw one of the bulbs into the lamp socket.
- Aim the lamp at the thermometer.
- Leave the light on for five minutes.
- Turn the light off and record the temperature.
- If you only have one desk lamp, wait until it cools before testing the next bulb.
- Create a chart to share your results. The chart should include the lumens, the wattage, and your recorded temperature for each bulb.
- Since all the bulbs are rated to provide the same amount of light, why does the amount of heat generated vary? Write a paragraph supporting your explanation.

Extensions:
- Find out how incandescent light bulbs work. Draw a diagram of an incandescent bulb and label its parts. Perform similar research for CFL and LED bulbs.
- Heat is energy. What medium conducted the energy from the light bulbs to the thermometer? (What happened to molecules between the lamp and the thermometer?)
- Write a review of the bulbs you tested. Recommend the best one for a study lamp. Use information you discovered in your experiment to provide reasons for your recommendation.

Resources for Teachers:
Light Bulbs and Lamps: Science Fair Projects
    https://www.juliantrubin.com/fairprojects/electricity/bulb.html
What Color Light Bulbs Give off the Most Heat?
    https://www.ehow.com/facts_6300458_color-bulbs-give-off-heat_.html
Shopping for Light Bulbs
    https://www.consumer.ftc.gov/articles/0164-shopping-light-bulbs

STEAM Skills:
Science: physics, energy, work, light, heat
Technology: investigating and comparing light bulb design
Engineering: studying light bulb design
Arts: writing a product review
Mathematics: temperature measurement, graphing, light measurement units, wattage

Bernoulli's Balloons and Paper Planes:
The Magic of Air Pressure

Objective: To demonstrate the effects of air pressure.

Materials:

Two round balloons   String   A drinking straw
Copy paper   Pencil

Student Procedure:

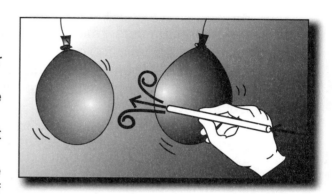

- Inflate the balloons and tie the ends shut.
- Tie a string to each balloon.
- Predict what will happen when you blow air between the balloons. Record your prediction.
- Use the straw to blow on the air between the balloons. Record the results.
- Explain what happened and why. (Use an Internet search to confirm your explanation.)
- Draw a three-panel comic strip illustrating the experiment. Use arrows to show the directions of air pressure in each panel.

Extensions:

- The same principle that pushes the balloons together helps planes fly. Use the Internet to see how an airplane wing uses air pressure to create lift. Draw a diagram of your own.

Science Fair Project Idea: Experiment with paper airplanes to create designs that travel farther, are faster, or do more loops. Draw diagrams to show the role of air pressure in your most successful designs.

Resources for Teachers:

Experimenting with Bernoulli's Principle
   http://scifun.chem.wisc.edu/HomeExpts/bernoulli.htm
Paper Airplane Designs
   https://www.foldnfly.com/#/1-1-1-1-1-1-1-1-2
How Do Airplanes Fly?
   https://www.youtube.com/watch?v=Gg0TXNXgz-w&vl=en
Bernoulli's Equation (advanced)
   https://www.grc.nasa.gov/WWW/k-12/airplane/bern.html

STEAM Skills:

Science: physics, air pressure, lift
Technology: researching flight
Engineering: researching airplane design
Arts: paper folding, drawing a comic strip, drawing a diagram
Mathematics: formulas, equations

The Periodic Table Code

Objective: To become familiar with the parts and functions of the Periodic Table.

Materials:

Copy of The Periodic Table   Paper

Student Procedure:

- A spaceship's crew is under heavy fire from an alien vessel. They have transmitted a message with the title "Periodic Test" and the following numbers. The numbers refer to the atomic numbers on the Periodic Table. Find the atomic numbers on the Periodic Table to decode the message. You will need the first letter of each chemical symbol.

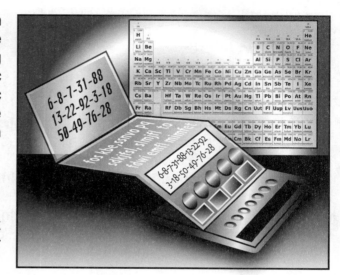

6-8-7-31-88-13-22-92-3-18-50-49-76-28

- Use the same code to write a message back to the crew. Trade messages with another member of your group and decipher it.

Extensions:

- Plan or make a slide show explaining the meaning of the symbols on The Periodic Table.
- Write a science fiction short story about the spaceship crew in this exercise. Make the Periodic Table Code an important part of the story.
- Write a paragraph explaining how colors make the Periodic Table more useful. Compare three different versions of the Table. Which is easiest to read? Which has the most information?

Resources for Teachers:

Royal Society of Chemistry's Interactive Periodic Table
   http://www.rsc.org/periodic-table
Los Alamos National Laboratory: Periodic Table of Elements
   http://periodic.lanl.gov/index.shtml
American Chemical Society: Elementary & Middle School Science Education Resources
   https://www.acs.org/content/acs/en/education/resources/k-8.html

STEAM Skills:

Science: chemistry, atomic structure, periodic table
Technology: using the Internet, using presentation software
Arts: writing science fiction, examining the use of color in charts
Mathematics: cryptology

Center of Attention: Model the Nucleus of Your Choice

Objective: To model the nucleus of an atom.

Materials:

Colored clay   Toothpicks   Black marker   Poster board or large paper
Optional: camera; computer with microphone and Internet connection; an individual, school, or class website

Student Procedure:

- Choose two colors of clay.
- Use a copy of The Periodic Table to find the atomic number for the element carbon. That will tell you how many positively charged protons to include in your nucleus.
- Represent the protons with clay balls. Make them all the same size and color.
- There are an equal number of neutrally charged neutrons. Make them slightly larger and use the other color of clay. Alternate protons and neutrons, arranging the particles in a ball held together with toothpicks.
- If time allows, repeat the procedure for the element helium and the element lithium.
- Optional: photograph your models and post results on an individual, school, or class website.

Extensions:

- Negatively charged electrons are found around the nucleus in orbitals or shells. Each electrically neutral element has the same number of electrons as protons. Electrons once were thought to move like planets orbiting the sun. Find out why many scientists stopped accepting that model.
- Find out what an isotope is. Explain the relationship between an isotope and an element. Use colored pencils to draw the nuclei of the three naturally occurring isotopes of hydrogen.
- Research ions. Explain what changes in an atom when it becomes an ion.

Resources for Teachers:

Atoms
    https://www.daytonastate.edu/asc/files/science120.pdf
The Development of the Atomic Model
    https://www.wired.com/2009/09/the-development-of-the-atomic-model/
Structure of the Atom
    https://www.nyu.edu/pages/mathmol/textbook/atoms.html
Guide to the Nuclear Wallchart
    http://www2.lbl.gov/abc/wallchart/outline.html
How to Find the Number of Protons, Neutrons, and Electrons!
    https://www.youtube.com/watch?v=auZvurPTCdM&feature=youtu.be
Why Don't Electrons Just Fall into the Nucleus of an Atom?
    https://io9.gizmodo.com/why-dont-electrons-just-fall-into-the-nucleus-of-an-ato-1597851164

STEAM Skills:

Science: chemistry, structure of the atom, isotopes, ions
Technology: using a camera, computer, and/or web page
Engineering: constructing a model
Arts: clay sculpture, scientific illustration
Mathematics: reading data from a chart

Ice to Steam: Timing Transformations

Objective: To observe and explain three phases (states) of matter.

Materials:

Pan   Hot plate or burner   Thermometer   Ice
Paper   Stopwatch or digital timer

Student Procedure:
- Put an ice cube in a pan. Measure the temperature of the ice.
- Place the pan over a heat source set to medium.
- Use the stopwatch or digital timer to keep track of how long it takes for the solid to become a liquid. Remove the pan and measure the temperature of the liquid. Record the results.
- Return the pan to the heat source. Keep track of the time it takes for the liquid to become a gas. When all the liquid is gone, remove the pan from the heat source and turn off the heat source.
- Explain the kind of energy you are adding to the ice in this experiment. Tell or show how you could slow down or increase the rate of phase change.
- Plan or make a display chart showing what happens to water molecules in the pan as ice changes to liquid and then to gas.

Extensions:
- Explain how freezing water in rock cracks causes physical weathering. Plan a poster showing this process.
- Make a diagram of a volcano showing three states of matter during an eruption.
- Investigate the process sculptors use to cast works of art in bronze. Explain the role states of matter play in their work.
- Find out how frozen carbon dioxide is used to create special effects in theater. Create a short slide show presenting your research.
- A fourth phase or state of matter is used in neon signs. It also occurs in space. It is called plasma. Write a sentence or two explaining the difference between gas and plasma.

Resources for Teachers:
Temperature Affects Matter Activities
    http://www.inquiryinaction.org/classroomactivities/topic.php?topic=Temperature%20Affects%20Matter
Three States of Matter
    https://courses.lumenlearning.com/introchem/chapter/three-states-of-matter/
States of Matter
    https://www.youtube.com/watch?v=HAPc6JH85pM
Matter: Definition and the Five States of Matter
    https://www.livescience.com/46506-states-of-matter.html

STEAM Skills:
Science: chemistry, volcanology, phases of matter, energy
Technology: heating, cooling, using the Internet, presentation software
Engineering: investigating container design, metal casting, and neon signs
Arts: bronze casting, dry-ice fog, scientific illustration
Mathematics: temperature measurement, time measurement

Layered Water: Salt Meets Fresh

Objective: To investigate the effects of differing water density.

Materials:

Clear plastic cups   Plastic spoons or coffee stirrers   Permanent marker
Salt   Water   Food coloring   Measuring teaspoon

Student Procedure:

- Label one cup SALT and the other cup FRESH.
- Fill each cup half-full of water.
- Add one teaspoon of salt to the cup labeled SALT.
- Stir the salt water to dissolve.
- Add a different color of food coloring to each cup. For example, you might add yellow to the salt water and blue to the freshwater.
- Predict what will happen when you mix them. Then pour the freshwater into the saltwater cup. Record what happens.
- Pour out the water and repeat the experiment, this time adding the salt water to the freshwater cup. Was the result the same? Explain why.
- If time allows, repeat the experiment with warm water, more salt, less salt, and any other variables you can think of.

Extensions:

- What new colors are created when the dyed waters mix? Do a watercolor painting reproducing the effect. Use a large brush to paint an even, wet yellow wash on watercolor paper. Wet your brush to remove most of the paint, then dip it into blue. Pull it across the top of the paper in one even stroke. Hold the paper up so the blue paint flows into the yellow. Lay it flat to dry. For more ideas, find works by Helen Frankenthaler.

Science Fair Project Idea:

- Investigate how the melting of polar ice will affect the salinity of ocean water and what this could mean for ocean currents.
- Use a smartphone, tablet, laptop, or other device to video this experiment. Add narration to explain what is happening and why.

Resources for Teachers:

Density of Ocean Water: https://www.windows2universe.org/earth/Water/density.html
Teachers: Go back to school with NOAA
    http://www.noaa.gov/stories/teachers-go-back-to-school-with-noaa
Saltwater is Denser Than Fresh Water by Doctor C https://youtu.be/gx3yNjd7jE0
Salt Water and Fresh Water http://scienceline.ucsb.edu/getkey.php?key=183

STEAM Skills:

Science: chemistry, water density, estuaries, melting ice caps
Technology: video production equipment and software
Arts: washes, color mixing, watercolor
Mathematics: measuring

Tea Painting: Soluble Color

Objective: To investigate the role of heat in solubility.

Materials:

Heat source and kettle   English Breakfast tea bags or other black tea
Rulers and pencils   Metal spoon and Pyrex measuring cup
Foam cup and plate   Watercolor paper   Watercolor brush

Student Procedure:

- Put a tea bag in a cup of cold water. Press it with the spoon. Observe what happens.
- Boil water and put another tea bag in the Pyrex measuring cup.
- Barely cover the bag with water. Press out as much color as possible with the spoon.
- Pour the tea into a foam cup and discard the bag.
- While the tea is cooling, use a ruler and pencil to make a mark on each edge of the paper one inch from the bottom. Draw a straight line between the marks, parallel to the bottom of the page. Add hills just above it. The landscape will be mostly sky.
- Pour a little of the tea onto your foam plate palette. Add a little water to dilute the solution. Paint the sky with this light color. Leave some white for clouds.
- Add more dark tea to the solution on your palette. Use it to paint the hills.
- Add a little more water. Paint the land below the horizon.

Extensions:

- Find out where the tea leaves get their dark brown color.
- Do a painting with instant coffee. Investigate how instant coffee is made.
- Try dissolving salt, chalk, flour, sand, and other common powders in both hot and cold water. Allow the water to evaporate from any solutions you create. What is left behind?
- Dissolve sugar in cold, warm, and hot water. Record the temperature of the water, the time needed to dissolve the sugar, and any residues in the bottom of the cup each time.

Science Fair Project Idea: Use heat to extract color from beets, red cabbage, and onion skins. Try tinting different kinds of fabric with natural dyes.

Resources for Teachers:

Solubility
    https://courses.lumenlearning.com/introchem/chapter/solubility/
How to Paint with Tea and Coffee
    https://www.ehow.com/how_6966291_paint-tea-coffee.html
Dye Like a Natural
    https://www.exploratorium.edu/snacks/dye-natural
Eating with Your Eyes: The Chemistry of Food Colorings
    https://www.acs.org/content/acs/en/education/resources/highschool/chemmatters/
    past-issues/2015-2016/october-2015/food-colorings.html

STEAM Skills:

Science: chemistry, solubility, heat energy
Technology: dyes, stains, tea and coffee manufacturing
Arts: landscapes, monochrome painting
Mathematics: measurement, parallel lines

Magic Paper: Acids and Bases

Objective: To create pH indicator strips and determine which liquids are acids, bases, or neutrals.

Materials:

Coffee filters, filter paper, or acid-free watercolor paper
Purple cabbage   Pan and strainer   Heat source
Acids: vinegar, lemon juice   Bases: dissolved baking soda, bleach

Procedure:

Teacher (in advance):

- Wash cabbage and cut it up.
- Cover with water and bring to a boil. Simmer between thirty minutes and an hour. Cool and strain the solution.

Students:

- Cut the filter paper into rectangular strips.
- Saturate them with prepared red cabbage juice. Then remove the strips and allow them to dry.
- Use these strips to test vinegar, lemon juice, dissolved baking soda, bleach, liquid dish soap, water, and other liquids. Bases will turn dark green and acids will turn red. Neutral substances will remain purple.
- Document the result of each test with a drawing. Use colored markers. Include the substance tested and the result. (Is the substance an acid, a base, or neutral?)

Extensions:

- Make indicator strips using bottled beet juice or the spice turmeric. Compare your results to the cabbage juice strips. Which works best?
- Compare your strips to commercial litmus paper. How do the results differ?
- Create a scale from acid to base using your results. Check the pH (potential hydrogen) level of each substance online. Label each substance tested.

Resources for Teachers:

Chemistry's Rainbow: Neutralize an Acid and a Base
    https://www.acs.org/content/dam/acsorg/education/outreach/kidschemistry/acids-and-bases-teachers-guide-chemistrys-rainbow.pdf
Classroom Resources: Acids & Bases
    https://teachchemistry.org/classroom-resources/topics/acids-bases?q%5Bgrade_level_ratings_grade_level_id_eq%5D=3

STEAM Skills:

Science: chemistry, acids and bases, solutions
Technology: using indicator strips
Engineering: making indicator strips
Arts: using colored markers to make a drawing, observing colors accurately
Mathematics: creating a scale, comparing pH levels, decimals

Mystery Powders: Chemical Changes

Objective: To investigate chemical changes.

Materials:

Eyedroppers or plastic spoons   Toothpicks (for mixing)
Straws (cut at an angle on the end)   Plastic cups to hold testing fluids
Black permanent markers   Moisture-resistant disposable plates
Testing fluids: water, vinegar, diluted iodine, indicator solution (red cabbage)
Powders: salt, cornstarch, baking soda, plaster of paris (each should be in a separate bag
  labeled with a number: 1-4)
***To establish proper lab procedure, caution students never to taste or smell any unknown
  substance and to wear the following:**   Plastic gloves   Goggles

Teacher Procedure: Present the following story:

When Detective Kim Ickal Chainj arrived at the bakery, the payroll cash was gone. An empty safe gaped open, but there were clues left behind. The safecracker had stepped in white powder and left his footprints. Just outside the door were the powdery prints of another person, the lookout. Forensics technicians found the footprints of a third suspect in the foreman's office beside the alarm box. In the parking lot was a fourth set of prints, those of the getaway driver.

When the suspects were captured, technicians analyzed their shoes. You have samples of the powders found. You will test each to discover how it reacts with water, vinegar, diluted iodine, and an indicator solution. The results will help detectives find out where each robber walked at the bakery.

Student Procedure:

- First, with the marker, divide your plate into four sections. Label them 1, 2, 3, and 4 to represent samples from the four shoes.
- Use a cut straw to scoop out and place four small piles of powder from bag 1 in the first section of your plate.
- Add a little water to the first pile and stir it with a toothpick. Record what happens.
- Add vinegar to the second pile. Stir it with a fresh toothpick. Record what happens.
- Try diluted iodine on the third pile. Record what happens.
- Use indicator solution on the last pile. Record what happens.
- Record each reaction carefully. Remember, the lack of a reaction is also a result.
- Repeat this procedure with each of the other three mystery powders.

Mystery Powders: Chemical Changes (Cont.)

Teacher: After students have recorded the results of their tests, present the following information:
- Salt dissolves in water but has little or no reaction with the other fluids. It doesn't fizz, change color, or harden.
- Baking soda fizzes slightly in water but fizzes vigorously in vinegar. It turns bluish with indicator solution because it's a base.
- Cornstarch darkens in the iodine solution, but there's little or no reaction with the other fluids.
- Plaster of paris hardens and heats up with water, but there is little or no change with the other fluids.
- **Note:** Dissolving salt is a physical change. As seen in a previous project, when the water evaporates, salt can be recovered, chemically unchanged. The other changes in this project are chemical changes.

Students: Name the powder on each robber's shoe.

*IMPORTANT: Dispose of all plates in the trash. Do not allow ANY plaster or plaster mixture to go down a drain. It will cause a permanent clog.

Extensions:
- Design a chart to make your results easy to read and understand. Include all the test findings.
- Test other powders such as powdered detergent, flour, sugar, and cornmeal. Make a poster or display to share your results.
- Use chemical change as a clue in an original mystery story or short play.
- Pour damp sand into a shoebox. Press a design into it using your fingers, spoons, or pencils. Mix plaster of paris and pour it over your design. Let the plaster set up and harden. Lift your casting out and display it.

Resources for Teachers:
Mystery Powders
  https://ngss.nsta.org/Resource.aspx?ResourceID=419
Chemical and Physical Changes
  http://www.mcwdn.org/chemist/pcchange.html
History of Mold Making and Casting
  https://smartartbox.com/blogs/smart-art-blog/history-of-mold-making-and-casting

STEAM Skills:
Science: chemistry, chemical change, physical change, observation
Technology: forensic chemistry
Engineering: studying the processes and applications of mold making
Arts: mystery writing, poster making, sand casting
Mathematics: measurement, creating a chart

Pounding Sand: Physical Changes

Objective: To investigate physical changes, as opposed to chemical changes.

Materials:

Loosely consolidated sandstone, siltstone, or mudstone (soft sedimentary rock, but not limestone)

Wooden boards capable of resisting pounding (or concrete outdoors)

Hammers or mallets   Goggles   Dust masks   Paper   Plastic jar   Water   Scale

Bucket to collect the waste water and rock powder

Student Procedure:

- Put on goggles and dust masks.
- Place a sheet of paper under the rock.
- Place the paper and rock on the scale. Record the weight.
- Pound the rock until it forms a powder.
- Explain how the rock has changed and why this is a physical rather than a chemical change.
- Place the paper holding the rock powder on the scale. Weigh it and record the weight. Compare it to the original weight of the rock. It should be the same. If it isn't, explain why. (There will be a physical explanation, such as wind blowing away particles.)
- Pick up the paper carefully and use it to pour the rock powder into the jar.
- Add water. Record your observations.
- Explain where or when you might see this happen in nature.
- Optional: Photograph or sketch each step of the project and create a slide show.

Caution: Do not pour the waste water down the drain. Pour it in the bucket provided.

Extensions:

- Impose as many different physical changes as you can on sheets of paper. Document the changes with photographs and create a display. (Examples: paper folding, crushing, painting, cutting, pulping)
- Plan a chart showing how rocks are broken up during commercial mining operations.
- Investigate how particle board or gypsum board is made. Explain which part of each process involves physical change and which involves chemical change.

Resources for Teachers:

Underground Mining
    https://www.greatmining.com/Hardrock-mining.html

What is Gypsum Board?
    https://www.gypsum.org/about/gypsum-101/gypsum-board/

Physical Changes
    https://www.bbc.com/bitesize/guides/zc9q7ty/revision/6

STEAM Skills:

Science: chemistry, physical changes, chemical changes

Technology: researching manufacturing gypsum board or particle board

Engineering: investigating techniques of breaking rock in commercial mining

Arts: paper art, photography, illustration

Mathematics: measuring weight

Describe the Suspect: Mineral Identification

Objective: To observe and test the physical properties of minerals to identify quartz and other minerals.

Materials:

Egg carton (for mineral samples—optional)
Marker   Magnifying glass
A numbered set of mineral samples including quartz, plus as many others as possible (talc, halite, calcite, muscovite, iron, pyrite, galena)
Streak plate (unglazed back of a porcelain tile)

Instructor Procedure: Present the following story:

A jewel robber owns a rock shop. His store contains large bins of mineral samples. Before he is captured, the robber sends an intercepted message to his partner. It's just one word: *quartz*. When detectives arrive, all labels are missing from the bins. They take a sample from each bin. Technicians test to find out which bin contains quartz, and the jewels.

Student Procedure:

• Examine the mineral samples in your kit. Use the properties listed below to identify the quartz.

Properties of Quartz

Conchoidal fracture
  (shell-like pattern; see sample fracture at right)
Colorless streak (makes no mark)
Glassy luster (not earthy, metallic, greasy, or silky)
Transparent or translucent
Hardness 7 (will scratch glass and most other minerals)

Extensions:

• Use color, fracture, luster, streak, and hardness to identify other minerals in the test kit.
• Write a detective story. Solve it with mineral identification.
• Use index cards to make a mineral identification reference deck. For each common mineral, include a photo and its properties.

Resources for Teachers:

Art's Mineral Identification Chart
   https://geology.com/minerals/mineral-identification.shtml
Mohs Hardness Test
   http://www.rocksandminerals.com/hardness/mohs.htm

STEAM Skills:

Science: earth science, minerals, properties, classification
Technology: using magnifying glass, streak plate
Engineering: designing tests to identify minerals
Arts: creative writing, graphic design

Can it Be Separated Ore Not?

Objective: To investigate methods of separating minerals from ores.

Materials:
    Computer
    Ore samples (iron, copper, bauxite)
    Product samples (aluminum cans, copper wire, stainless steel spoons)

Student Procedure:

- Choose an object.
- Search online to discover the source of the metal it contains.
- Use online information to match the metal product to one of the provided ore samples.
- Design a table display showing the steps commercial mining operations use to extract the mineral from its ore. As part of your display, include a bar graph showing the sources, by nation, of the mineral you chose.

Extensions:
- Create a short video explaining the process of extracting a mineral from its ore. It could be one of the three in this project or another mineral that interests you.
- Find out about the alloy used to wrap guitar strings. Which minerals are used to make it? Why is it used?
- Design a display showing the sources of metals used in U.S. coins.
- Produce a slide show, including statistics, graphs, and images, to convince people that recycling aluminum cans is important.

Resources for Teachers:
Cookie Mining
    http://www.earthsciweek.org/classroom-activities/cookie-mining
What Are the Main Methods of Mining?
    https://www.americangeosciences.org/critical-issues/faq/what-are-main-mining-methods
Dig into Mining: The Story of Copper
    http://www.digintomining.com/middle-school-resources

STEAM Skills:
Science: earth science, minerals, economics
Technology: manufacturing, metallurgy, computer research, video equipment and presentation software
Engineering: researching mining and manufacturing
Arts: display design, music, video presentation
Mathematics: statistics, graphing

Graham Cracker Tectonics

Objective: To model plate tectonics.

Materials:

Whole graham crackers
Cup of water
Waxed paper
Cake frosting
Plastic knives

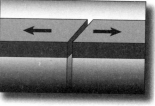

Divergent

Student Procedure:

> The earth's crust consists of pieces (**plates**) sitting on top of the **asthenosphere** (upper mantle). These plates move away from each other (**divergent**) or toward each other (**convergent**). They can also slide past each other (**transform**).

Convergent

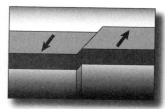

Transform

- To model a **divergent continental plate boundary**, spread a thin, even layer of frosting on the waxed paper. Break the cracker in half. Place the pieces side by side on top of the frosting. Pressing down on both crackers, push them slowly apart (not more than a centimeter.) Observe and record what happens.
- To model a **convergent continental plate boundary**, prepare the waxed paper base with frosting. Break one half of the cracker in half. Dip one end of each quarter in water to soften. Place the crackers, soft ends together, on top of the frosting. Push them toward each other slowly. Observe and record what happens.

Extensions:

- Video a friend creating each model. Write a script explaining how a similar process takes place along plate boundaries on earth.
- Use graham crackers and frosting to model a transform plate boundary.

Resources for Teachers:

Understanding Plate Motions
  htttps://pubs.usgs.gov/gip/dynamic/understanding.html
How Many Plates?
  http://www.mantleplumes.org/WebDocuments/DLAHowManyPlates.pdf
Slip, Slide, Collide
  http://www.open.edu/openlearn/science-maths-technology/slip-slide-collide

STEAM Skills:

Science: earth science, plate tectonics
Technology: video production, online research
Engineering: creating plate models
Arts: script writing, creating models

It Is Your Fault: Faults and Folds in Clay

Objective: To model faults and folds.

Materials:
    Craft clay or dough in several colors
    Rolling pin or large-diameter dowel
    Plastic knife
    Computer with Internet connection

Student Procedure:

- Roll or press out flat strips of each color of clay to represent rock strata.
- Stack the strips.
- Bend the stack of "rock layers." (Do not fold tightly.)
- Photograph or sketch the result.
- Repeat with another set of strips. This time, lay the stack on a table with the edges of the layers facing up. Cut the layered strip in half at an angle. Slide one half upwards along the cut (fault.) Photograph or sketch the result.
- What forces could cause rock layers to bend or break like this? Record your ideas.
- Online, find photographs of folded and faulted rock layers.

Extensions:
- Find public-domain photographs of faults and folds online. Use them, along with photos or sketches of your models, to create a slide show. Record a narration explaining how folds and faults happen and how they affect people.
- Research the ways engineers plan for fault movement when designing a dam, bridge, or building.

Resources for Teachers:
Faulty Movement
    https://www.teachengineering.org/activities/view/cub_natdis_lesson02_activity3
USGS Educational Resources for Secondary Grades (7–12)
    https://education.usgs.gov/secondary.html

STEAM Skills:
Science: earth science, stratigraphy, plate tectonics
Technology: online research, slide show production
Engineering: researching earthquake-resistant architecture, creating layered models
Arts: photography, sketching, writing narration

Fossil Detectives: Reading the Clues

Objective: To reconstruct the order of rock layers based on fossils.

Materials:

Photographs of trilobites, brachiopods, ammonites, graptolites, and mammal or bird skeletons
8 x 10 sheets of corrugated cardboard or foam core   Glue   Markers

Student Procedure:

- Glue one fossil photograph to the front of each board.
- Write the fossil's name and when it lived on the back.
- Use the chart below to arrange the rock layers in order with the oldest layer on the bottom.

Index Fossils		
Fossil Name	**Fossil Illustration**	**Years (before the present) it lived**
Mammals (dog)		Cenozoic Era, 65 million years ago to today
Graptolites		510 million years ago to 320 million years ago
Ammonites		240 million years ago to 65 million years ago
Mucrospirifer Brachiopods		410 million years ago to 359 million years ago
Trilobites		521 million years ago to 252 million years ago

Extensions:

- Add additional boards using information from online Index Fossil charts.
- Play a game with friends. Scatter the boards around the room. Players assemble the layers in order with the oldest on the bottom and youngest on top. Score extra points by explaining how the layers were mixed up. (folding, faulting, erosion)

Resources for Teachers:

Index Fossils
   https://pubs.usgs.gov/gip/geotime/fossils.html
Law of Superimposition
   https://www.britannica.com/science/law-of-superposition

STEAM Skills:

Science: earth science, fossils, paleobiology
Technology: Internet research
Arts: assembling fossil layers
Mathematics: large numbers (age of fossils), negative numbers

How Far to the Hadean? Geologic Time on the Quad

Objective: To create a geologic time scale.

Materials:

Geologic time chart from a current text, encyclopedia, or the Internet
Adding machine tape
Pencil
Ruler
Laminated pages with details about one geologic era on each. Add a colored page for the extinction of the dinosaurs and another for the beginning of recorded history.
Rolling measuring tool, tape measure, or other measuring device
A basketball court, 84 feet

Student Procedure:

- Measure off 84 inches of adding machine tape.
- Each inch of tape will represent about 55 million years of geologic time.
  (4,600,000,000 years divided by 84 inches or 84 feet, rounded off)
- Mark and label eras and major events in geologic history. You will need to use fractions of an inch.

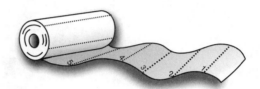

Extensions:

- Create an illustration for each geologic era or event.
- Use your illustrations or laminated signs to mark off geologic eras and events on the school basketball court. Your plan will help. Each inch of the tape will equal a foot on the court.
- Design a geologic timeline display for the hallway, the side of the building, or another area on campus. Use a calculator or computer to scale geologic time to your available space.

Resources for Teachers:

Paleontology: It's a Matter of Time (Petrified Forest National Park)
    https://www.nps.gov/pefo/learn/education/classrooms/upload/paleo_lesson3.pdf
How Science Figured Out the Age of Earth
    https://www.scientificamerican.com/article/how-science-figured-out-the-age-of-the-earth/

STEAM Skills:

Science: earth science, geologic time
Technology: calculators, measuring devices
Engineering: planning the time scale so it fits the space provided
Arts: scientific illustration
Mathematics: scale, proportion, measurement, large numbers, rounding off, fractions

Settling: Making Sediments

Objective: To create and observe sedimentary layers.

Materials:

2 plastic jars
Fine gravel
Chalk dust

Different colors of sand
Coarse gravel
Water

Tub or bucket to catch overflow

Student Procedure:

- Fill the jar with water.
- Set it inside a tub or bucket to catch any overflow.
- Add each type of sand, gravel, or dust in random order.
- Let each layer settle before adding the next.
- Explain how this kind of deposition happens in nature.
- Fill the second jar with water.
- Set it inside a tub or bucket to catch any overflow.
- Add all the sediment types at once.
- Observe what happens. Are the results the same or different? Why do you think this happened? When would this kind of deposition happen in nature?
- How would this kind of sedimentation affect dams? How would engineers deal with the problem? Record your ideas in a science journal.

Extensions:

- Find and photograph sedimentary rock layers in your neighborhood or town.
- Find photographs of sedimentary rock layers online.
- How are rock layers in nature the same or different from those in your experiment?
- Plan or prepare a display of different types of sedimentary rocks.
- In a dry jar, use colored sands to create a layered sand design.

Resources for Teachers:

Pictures of Sedimentary Rocks
   https://geology.com/rocks/sedimentary-rocks.shtml
How to Color Sand
   https://www.wikihow.com/Color-Sand
How to Do Sand Art
   https://www.ehow.com/how_4457088_do-sand-art.html

STEAM Skills:

Science: earth science, stratigraphy, deposition
Technology: using a camera
Engineering: researching dam sedimentation, dredging
Arts: colored sand designs, photography

Salts of the Earth: Evaporites

Objective: To grow crystals through evaporation.

Materials:

    Baking soda (borax, table salt, or alum)
    Plastic cups (or jars), spoons, and pencils
    6" lengths of cotton string and paper clips
    Hot tap water
    Magnifying glass

Student Procedure:
- Tie one end of the string to the middle of a pencil.
- Tie the other end to a paperclip. Drop the paperclip into the cup. Balance the pencil across the top. If the hanging string bunches up on the bottom of the cup, shorten it.
- Remove the pencil and string while filling the cup with hot tap water.
- Add baking soda, a spoonful at a time, until it stops dissolving.
- Put the cup where it won't be disturbed and replace the string.
- Using a camera or sketches, document what happens over the next few days.
- Optional: Prepare additional cups using table salt, alum, or borax (without detergent).
  *Warning: Borax and alum can be toxic. Use gloves and goggles. Do not ingest. Avoid boiling water.

Extensions:
- Create a display showing how baking soda, borax, and salt were formed, how they are mined, how they are used, or how much they add to the economy each year.
- Make a model salt flat in a disposable aluminum pie pan using water, dirt, salt, and baking soda. Create realistic layers.
- Allow seawater or other brackish water to evaporate in a disposable container. Use magnification to observe and sketch the crystals left behind.

Resources for Teachers:
Solubility Science: How to Grow the Best Crystals
    https://www.scientificamerican.com/article/bring-science-home-crystals/
How to Make Borax Crystal Snowflakes | Holiday Science Project
    https://www.livescience.com/41636-borax-crystal-snowflakes.html
Evaporite Environment
    https://www.amnh.org/exhibitions/permanent-exhibitions/harry-frank-guggenheim-hall-of-minerals/mineral-forming-environments/evaporite-environment

STEAM Skills:
Science: earth science, evaporites, solutions, chemistry, saturation, crystallography
Technology: mining of precipitates, modeling of salt flat, using magnifying glass
Engineering: researching mining of precipitates
Arts: photography, sketching
Mathematics: geometric crystal shapes, graphs

Hot Rock Soup: Create a Picture Book

Objective: To understand and explain the formation of igneous rocks

Materials:

5 sheets of copy paper per participant
Colored pencils
A long-arm stapler
Internet access, reference books, or science texts

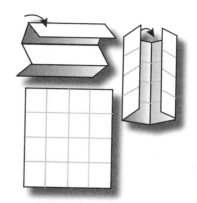

Student Procedure:

- Fold one sheet of paper twice in each direction creating 16 sections. This is your book map. Each section is a page.
- You will create a picture book showing second-graders how igneous rocks are formed.
- Use the book map to decide what information goes on each page.
- Note important words and concepts. Plan lots of pictures. Include data such as the melting temperature of rock. (Your audience loves big numbers.)
- To make the actual book, fold four sheets of copy paper in half. Number the pages in the book map and your book, then get to work.
- Fasten the finished pages at the fold with a long-arm stapler.
- Create an exciting front cover. It should include your title, your name, and an interesting picture.
- Share your book with primary students at a local school.

Extensions:

- Create picture books about other earth science topics such as crystals, erosion, mineral identification, or fossils.
- Use the art for your picture book to create a slide presentation. Record your text as the narration.
- Design a museum-style display of igneous rocks. Include a self-checking way for viewers to match each rock with information about its origin.

Resources for Teachers:

Pictures of Igneous Rocks
  https://geology.com/rocks/igneous-rocks.shtml
What are Igneous Rocks?
  https://www.usgs.gov/faqs/what-are-igneous-rocks?qt-news_science_products=0#qt-news_science_products

STEAM Skills:

Science: earth science, igneous rocks, volcanology, rock types
Technology: Internet research, slide presentation
Engineering: designing a book, designing an interactive display
Arts: illustrating concepts, scientific illustration, book and display design
Mathematics: temperature measurement

Mudslide! Erosion Run Amuck

Objective: To design solutions mitigating mudslide danger.

Materials:
Photographs of a recently burned slope with structures at the bottom
Photographs of streambeds with bridges after an extensive fire
Photographs of mudslide damage and flooding due to erosion
Internet access

Student Procedure:
- Examine photographs of burn damage.
- Predict what will happen when heavy rains fall after natural groundcover has been destroyed.
- Use the Internet to find data about property losses and loss of life due to mudslides after fires.
- Design a way to protect a structure shown in a post-fire photograph from potential damage or destruction in a mudslide.
- Present your solution as a drawing or a model.
- If there has been a mudslide or other erosion damage on or near your campus, photograph it. Document any efforts that the community has made to clean it up or prevent it from happening again.
- Come up with a new solution. Present it in a report with diagrams or with a model.

Extensions:
- Perform research in the library or online to see whether your solution to the problem has been tried and whether it succeeded.
- Create a model demonstrating with actual water and soil how your solution could protect the structure.
- Are there places where people should not build houses or commercial structures? Why or why not? Write an opinion piece for a local newspaper supporting your point of view. Use statistics to support your points.

Resources for Teachers:
How to Reduce the Effects of a Landslide
  http://www.wlf2.org/how-to-reduce-the-effects-of-a-landslide/
Landslides & Debris Flow
  https://www.ready.gov/landslides-debris-flow

STEAM Skills:
Science: earth science, ecology, plant science, erosion, mudflows
Technology: Internet research, use of materials to build mudflow damage mitigation system model
Engineering: designing mudflow damage mitigation systems
Arts: writing a persuasive essay, designing effective diagrams
Mathematics: using statistics to support an argument, documenting economic impacts of natural disasters

Soil Profile in a Jar

Objective: To model the interaction of inorganic and organic materials in the development of soil.

Materials:

Transparent plastic jars or cups, plastic gloves
Self-stick labels   Markers
Collecting bags and a trowel (if students collect the following materials)
A flat rock (fits inside the bottom of the jar), medium gravel, sand, loose soil, humus or dead plant materials, grass in soil.

Student Procedure:

- If possible, visit a location (on or adjacent to campus) with a visible soil profile. Observe and photograph it.
- Gather most of the materials needed for the model on campus (or bring them from home).
- If an outdoor tour is not possible, find photos of soil horizons online. The instructor will provide garden center basics: flat rocks, gravel, sandy garden soil, soil mixed with humus, dark humus, and turf.
- Create layers in the container with larger rocks on the bottom, sandy soil in the middle, then dark humus and living plants on top.
- Apply labels to the jar to mark each layer. From top to bottom these would be O (organic), A (mostly mineral with some organic material), B (subsoil), and C (rocks).
- Make a chart to accompany your model soil profile. Explain why each layer is important and tell how it formed.

Extensions:

- Around the world, we are losing top soils. Research the reasons for this loss. Design a method to preserve top soil. Use statistics to support your solution.

Resources for Teachers:

Losing Ground
   https://www.fewresources.org/soil-science-and-society-were-running-out-of-dirt.html
Topsoil Erosion
   http://large.stanford.edu/courses/2015/ph240/verso2/

STEAM Skills:

Science: earth science, life science, ecology, erosion
Technology: researching agriculture
Engineering: propose a system design for preserving topsoil
Arts: visual presentation of information
Mathematics: using statistical trends to make predictions

Sorting Things Out: Exploring Taxonomy

Objective: To use dichotomous keys in the process of identification.

Materials:

Paper
Colored pencils
Pictures of different kinds of trees with bark and leaf detail for each.
A sample dichotomous identification key (online or in a text)

Student Procedure:

You have just landed on the forest planet Arg. Only seeds of the Aplee tree are edible. All others are toxic. Make a dichotomous identification key to help others in your party identify the Aplee. Here's the information you will need:

> ### Common Trees on Planet Arg
> Mishmark: A 25+ ft. tree with blue leaves and rough bark
> Rutgack: A 25+ ft. tree with pink leaves and smooth bark
> Larmler: A 25+ ft. tree with pink leaves and rough bark
> Aplee: A 15 ft. tree with pink leaves and rough bark

Extensions:

• Draw each tree. Include a closeup of bark detail, a leaf, and a cone or seedpod.
• Expand your dichotomous key by adding other imaginary trees. Additional characteristics could include seeds or cones, leaf shapes, and location (hillside or near water).
• Write a story about a colony or exploration party on Arg.
• Make a dichotomous identification key for trees or shrubs on your school campus or trees native to your community. Share it with the school or local library.
• Design an online tool for identifying the trees on Arg.
• Use metric measures (meters) instead of the Imperial system (feet) on your dichotomous key.

Resources for Teachers:

Classify It!
    http://sciencenetlinks.com/lessons/classify-it/
Common Trees of the Pacific Northwest
    https://oregonstate.edu/trees/dichotomous_key.html

STEAM Skills:

Science: plant science, taxonomy, dendrology, dichotomous keys
Technology: Web design
Arts: speculative fiction writing, imaginative drawing
Mathematics: measurement, scale drawings

Drawing From Life: Sketching a Plant Cell

Objective: To observe parts of a plant cell.

Materials:

Onion skins   Iodine   Tweezers
Blank microscope slides (or prepared plant cell slides)
Microscope   Colored pencils   Paper

Student Procedure:

- Make onion skin slides (find directions online) or use prepared slides.
- Observe plant cells through the microscope.
- Draw a single cell as accurately as you can.
- Use the diagram below to help you to label the parts of your cell.

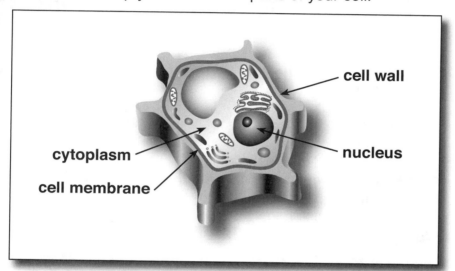

Extensions:

- Create slides for other kinds of plant cells. Draw them. How are they the same or different?
- Design a display explaining the purpose of each part of a plant cell.

Resources for Teachers:

How to Prepare an Onion Cell Slide
    https://en.wikibooks.org/wiki/School_Science/How_to_prepare_an_onion_cell_slide
Plant Cell Parts
    https://biologywise.com/plant-cell-parts

STEAM Skills:

Science: plant science, biology, botany, cell structure
Technology: using a microscope, researching online
Engineering: creating a microscope slide
Arts: scientific illustration

The Guy With Green Hair: Playing With Photosynthesis

Objective: To explore the effects of light on green plants.

Materials:

Foam cups	Marker	Garden soil or planter mix	Thermometer
Grass seed	Water	Paper	Measuring cup

Student Procedure:

Preparation:
- Draw a face on one side of each cup.
- Give each cup a silly name and write it on the back.
- Fill the cups with soil.
- Plant grass seed in the soil and add water.
- Place the cups in a warm, well-lit window. Keep damp.

Experiment: (after the grass has grown)
- Leave some cups in the sunlight.
- Place some cups in a closet or dark place.
- Scatter other cups in lit parts of the room, but not near the window.
- Predict what will happen and record your predictions.
- After a week, compare the cups. Record the results.
- Move the cups. Place the ones from the closet near the window and the ones from the window in the closet. Leave them for another week.
- Keep all the cups warm and the soil equally damp.
- Observe and explain your results.

Extensions:
- Create a chart or illustration showing how most animal life depends on photosynthesis.
- Place plants under different-colored light bulbs and compare results.
- Use the Internet to find life forms that do not depend on photosynthesis. Explain what these life forms mean for the possible existence of life on other planets.

Resources for Teachers:
What is Photosynthesis?
  https://ssec.si.edu/stemvisions-blog/what-photosynthesis
Life Science: Middle School Biology (Carlsbad Caverns National Park)
  https://www.nps.gov/cave/learn/education/upload/biology_middle_school.pdf

STEAM Skills:
Science: plant science, biology, botany, photosynthesis, ecology, experimental design
Technology: using different light bulbs, using the Internet to research life forms
Arts: visual communication
Mathematics: measurement (temperature, water, plant growth)

White Carnations Suck: Capillary Action

Objective: To investigate capillary action.

Materials:

Water   Clear plastic cups   Heavy paper towels
Scissors   Food coloring
White carnations (or celery stalks with fresh leaves)

Student Procedure:

- Add a drop of food coloring to the water (Cup should be less than a quarter full.)
- Cut a piece of heavy paper towel or blotter paper in strips. Place one end of the strip in colored water. Observe what happens. Why is this surprising? (Gravity?)
- Slice the end of the flower stem or celery stalk so there is a fresh cut.
- Place the end of the stem or stalk in the colored water. (Add a little more water and color if necessary.)
- Observe what happens.

Extensions:

- Create a slide presentation to show why capillary action is important for plants. Draw diagrams or use public domain images from the Internet.
- Photograph each step of the investigations on this page. Print the photos and use them to create a display.
- Dip paper towels in colored water to create dyed designs.
  https://craftprojectideas.com/tie-dyed-paper-towel-experiment/

Resources for Teachers:

Lighting Up Leaves (Science Friday)
  https://youtu.be/Gps8uktGtFY
Capillary Action
  https://water.usgs.gov/edu/capillaryaction.html

STEAM Skills:

Science: plant science, botany, capillary action
Technology: photography, presentation software
Arts: presentation design, capillary action in water media

Seed Conspirators: Distribution Strategies

Objective: To investigate seed distribution strategies.

Materials:
Collecting box and plastic bags for samples
Latex or other gloves to use while collecting samples
Stick-on labels to record locations where samples were found
Markers or pens for labeling
Landscaped or natural outdoor area on school campus with trees, shrubs, grasses, and flowers (best in autumn in most areas)
Or seed samples gathered by the instructor and stored for this investigation, with photographs of source plants.
Or plant science text, an encyclopedia, or the Internet

Student Procedure:
- With the group at school, or with your family at home, gather samples of seed pods from trees, shrubs, and grasses. **Caution: It is best to use gloves when collecting samples in case the plants could induce an allergic reaction.**
- Create a label for each sample before placing it in a plastic bag. On the label, number the sample, record the date, and give the location.
- If possible, photograph the source tree or plant, along with the sample.
- Design a display to share your samples, along with ways these seeds would be distributed. Common means of distribution include wind (dandelion seeds), bird or animal scat, sticking to animal fur, gravity, and water.
- If you cannot collect seeds, design your display using provided samples or public domain photographs from the Internet.

Extensions:
- Use research sources such as a text, the library, or the Internet to name the plants in your display. Add interesting facts about them.
- Find out how and why fruit, vegetable, and grain seeds are genetically engineered. Explain why this is controversial.

Resources for Teachers:
Gone with the Wind: Plant Seed Dispersal
   https://www.scientificamerican.com/article/gone-with-the-wind-plant-seed-dispersal/
Seed Dispersal
   https://calscomm.cals.cornell.edu/naturalist/Naturalist-Outreach-Seed-dispersal.pdf

STEAM Skills:
Science: plant science, sample collection, seed dispersal
Technology: Internet research, recording information with a camera
Engineering: researching genetically engineered seeds
Arts: display design

In Another Vein: Leaf Prints

Objective: To observe the structure of various kinds of leaves.

Materials:

Leaves   Paper   Tempera paint   Paint brushes
Optional: Pencils, crayons, charcoal, oil pastels
Optional: Seed pods or other natural found objects

Student Procedure:

- Bring five different kinds of leaves from home or gather them on the school campus with the class.
- Sketch each leaf.
- Use print or Internet reference materials to identify the tree.
- Write a short description explaining how each leaf helps the tree adapt to its environment. For example, a needle shape allows wind to pass through and helps the tree retain more water.
- Choose one leaf to print.
- Paint the rougher side of the leaf with tempera.
- Press it onto the paper.
- There will be paint remaining on the leaf. Press it again on another part of the paper or apply more paint in a different color. If you plan to use more than one color, use the lightest value (yellow) for your first print and add colors with darker values. For example, your second print might be red and your last might be blue.
- Turn the leaf in different directions and don't be afraid to overlap your prints.

Extensions:

- Use frottage (rubbing) to capture the vein structure and shape of leaves collected at home or on campus. Try it with pencils, crayons, charcoal, or oil pastels.
- Make tempera paint prints using seed pods or other natural found objects.

Resources for Teachers:
Nature Printing
   https://en.wikipedia.org/wiki/Nature_printing
Art Term: Frottage
   https://www.tate.org.uk/art/art-terms/f/frottage
The Secret Math of Plants
   http://newsroom.ucla.edu/releases/ucla-biologists-discover-new-mathematical-249097

STEAM Skills:
Science: plant science, leaf structure and function
Technology: using the Internet to identify trees
Arts: printmaking, frottage, color combination
Mathematics: observing numbers associated with leaves (number of leaflets, veins, etc.)

Putting Down Roots: A Function and Variety Slide Show

Objective: To observe or research and explain the structure and function of various roots.

Materials:

Internet connection or library
Computer
Slide presentation software
Optional: Avocado pit, carrots with leafy tops, containers, water, potting soil

Student Procedure:

- Online, find public domain photographs of different kinds of roots.
- Show how roots both anchor the plant and provide nutrients, oxygen, and water to the plant. Some kinds of roots also store carbohydrates for future growth. Show some examples.
- Demonstrate how the type of soil and water table influence the way tree roots grow.
- Use presentation software to create a slide show. Write and record narration to accompany the slides.

Extensions:

- Grow an avocado tree from a pit.
    https://www.californiaavocado.com/avocado101/your-own-avocado-tree
- Create an indoor garden using carrot tops.
    http://www.birdsandblooms.com/blog/indoor-garden-project-using-carrot-tops/

Resources for Teachers:

Plant-Soil Interactions (Grades 6-8)
    https://www.agclassroom.org/teacher/matrix/lessonplan.cfm?lpid=229
Root Adaptations
    https://www.montclair.edu/csam/prism/rainforest-connection/australia/root-adaptations/
Root Types
    http://www.backyardnature.net/roottype.htm

STEAM Skills:

Science: plant science, adaptations, carbohydrate storage
Technology: using presentation software, using video and audio equipment
Arts: presentation design

A Dissected Still-Life: Looking Into Flowers

Objective: To observe the parts of a flower through dissection.

Materials:

Lilies or tulips (hibiscus, daffodils, or gladiolus also work)   Magnifying glasses
Tweezers   A metric ruler   Colored pencils   Paper
Cutting tools or dissection kits   Internet access, text, or reference books

Student Procedure:

- Draw the parts of the flower from the side and the top before removing or cutting anything.
- Gently remove one or two petals to reveal the structure inside. Draw this view.
- Label each of the following parts with a number: petal, stem, pistil, stigma, style, stamen, filament, anther
- On a lined notebook page, create a key for your drawing. List each numbered part on a separate line.
- Carefully remove each part from the blossom and measure it (in millimeters, mm). Add this information to your key.
- Add a phrase or short sentence to each item in the key, explaining the function of that flower part.
- Use the best available cutting tool to dissect the ovary to reveal the ovules.
- Add a close-up sketch of the dissected ovary to a corner of your flower drawing. Number this and add the information to your key.

Extensions:

- Dissect other flowers. Explain why not all flowers are equally useful for this project.
- Make a scientific drawing of a local tree or other plant with a key. Label all parts and their functions.

Resources for Teachers:

Plantenstein is the Suspect
  https://extension.illinois.edu/gpe/case4/c4facts1a.html
Origami Tulip
  https://www.youtube.com/watch?v=na4XF5zVn6w
Botanical Art and Artists: Scientific Botanical Illustration
  https://www.botanicalartandartists.com/scientific-botanical-illustration.html

STEAM Skills:

Science: plant science, flowering plants, dissection
Technology: researching using computers and the Internet
Arts: botanical illustration
Mathematics: measurement

Find Two the Same: Natural Variability

Objective: To explore the phenomenon of natural variability

Materials:

Groups of up to 20 of any of the following: pine cones; pumpkin seeds; dried pinto beans; sunflower seeds in the shell; peanuts in the shell; pistachios in the shell; walnuts, pecans, or almonds in the shell; leaves from the same tree; seedpods from the same tree or bush

Magnifying glasses
Paper
Colored pencils
Ruler

Student Procedure:

• Examine a group of similar nuts, seeds, or leaves.
• Make a chart showing which characteristics the items share and which characteristics vary.
• Select two items that are most alike.
• Measure both.
• Draw careful sketches of each side by side. Use a magnifying glass to check your details.

Extensions:

• Repeat this project with twice as many seeds or leaves or a different type of seed or leaf. Document your results. Compare your results with your original observations.
• Write a few paragraphs about the advantages of natural variations in plants.
• Photograph different individuals of the same species of local tree, bush, or cactus. Create a slide show or display highlighting their differences.
• Create a display showing how natural variation has helped humans develop food crops.

Resources for Teachers:

Why Plant 'Clones' Aren't Identical
    https://www.sciencedaily.com/releases/2011/08/110804212931.htm
Natural Variation in Plants
    https://www.nature.com/subjects/natural-variation-in-plants
What Has Natural Variation Taught Us about Plant Development, Physiology, and Adaptation?
    http://www.plantcell.org/content/21/7/1877

STEAM Skills:

Science: plant science, genetics, variability, seeds
Technology: using a camera and slide presentation software or equipment
Engineering: researching food crop development
Arts: botanical illustration, informational writing
Mathematics: measurement, charts and graphs

Algae on Your Table: A Chart

Objective: To demonstrate the uses of algae in common foods.

Materials:

Paper plates Markers Computers and the Internet

Student Procedure:

- Use search terms to find "algae in foods"
- List some of the foods that contain algae.
- Draw a line dividing the paper plate in half.
- On one side, draw the kinds of algae most commonly used in foods. Label them with their Latin names.
- On the other half, draw some of the products containing algae. Label this half with names used for products made with algae used in food.
- On a separate paper, make a chart showing the sources of food-grade algae, the amount grown or harvested each year, and the value of the crop.

Extensions:

- Write a science fiction story using what you have learned about algae. For example, it could be about a future time when food sources have been destroyed and people live on insects and algae.
- Make a display showing the health benefits of different types of algae.
- The use of algae in some foods is controversial. Stage a panel discussion. Each participant should become an "expert" on one point of view and defend it.
- Create a slide show explaining the importance of marine algae to the ecosystem, including the atmosphere and the biosphere.
- Make a display including examples of algae you have grown. Develop an experiment showing how different conditions (light, moisture, temperature) affect its growth and development.

Resources for Teachers:

The Great Algae Race
   https://www.teachengineering.org/activities/view/usf_biorecycling_lesson01_activity2
The Algae-in-a-Bottle Experiment: A High-Impact Learning Activity
   https://serc.carleton.edu/sp/activities/124605.html
Using Toxic Algal Blooms to Teach Structure and Function
   http://nstacommunities.org/blog/2018/10/24/using-toxic-algal-blooms-to-teach-structure-and-function/
K-12 Algae Stem Initiative
   http://thealgaefoundation.org/K-12_initiative.html

STEAM Skills:

Science: plant science, algae
Technology: food technology, presentation software
Engineering: improving food texture, planning for food scarcity, designing algae growth experiment
Arts: designing displays, writing speculative fiction, writing nonfiction
Mathematics: designing charts and graphs to make data accessible

Your Favorite Biome: A Collage

Objective: To research and show plants and animals in a particular biome.

Materials:

Large sheet of drawing or watercolor paper   Scissors   Paste, glue, or glue sticks
Nature, travel, or other magazines (or brochures) with plant and animal photographs

Student Procedure:

- Select your favorite biome. It could be a Pacific Ocean shore, a polar sea, a southwestern desert, a northeastern forest, a local stream valley, or something else.
- Consult reference books or the Internet to find out which plants and animals live together in your chosen biome.
- Find and cut out photographs of plants and animals. Images are also available on the Internet.
- Arrange the pictures to fill the large sheet of paper. Aim for a pleasing design rather than a literal landscape. The photos will be different sizes. A squirrel might be larger than a pine tree. For this collage, it doesn't matter.
- On a sheet of blank copy paper, make a chart showing annual precipitation, temperature, seasonal variations, soil conditions, and other non-biological factors in the area where your biome is located.
- Glue the copy paper to the back of your collage and print the name of the biome above it.

Extensions:

- Take photos of a local biome. List as many plants and animals as you can identify. The local chapter of The National Audubon Society or other wildlife organization may be able to help.
- Make an identification card set for a biome. Include illustrations, pictures, and facts for as many plants and animals as possible.
- Write a fantasy story set in a real or imagined biome. Use predator/prey relationships, climate, and other factors to make your setting realistic. You can include talking animals or even plants if you want to.
- Find out how some companies are working to do petroleum and mineral extraction with minimum disruption to local biomes.

Resources for Teachers:

Biomes of the World
  https://www.teachersfirst.com/lessons/biomes/
Biomes
  https://www.pbslearningmedia.org/resource/tdc02.sci.life.eco.lp_biomes/biomes/
Life Science Middle School Ecology
  https://www.nps.gov/cave/learn/education/upload/ecology_ms_biosphere.pdf
NASA Earth Observatory: Teacher Resources
  https://earthobservatory.nasa.gov/experiments/biome/teacherresource.php

STEAM Skills:

Science: animal science, life sciences, ecology, biomes
Technology: Internet research, photography
Engineering: researching methods to harvest resources with minimum environmental impact
Arts: collage, writing a fantasy story, illustration
Mathematics: charting precipitation, temperature, and other data

The Secret Life of Dragonflies: A Folded Life Cycle Book

Objective: To research animal life cycles.

Materials:

Access to the Internet or reference books   Copy paper   Scissors   Ruler
Tape or glue   Pencils   Colored pencils   Fine markers or black pens
Yarn, ribbon, or string

Student Procedure:

- Research the life cycle of a dragonfly. List the phases of its life, noting the average length of time the creature spends in each, where it lives then, and what it eats.
- Fold a sheet of copy paper to create a book map. Each square will represent a page in your finished book.
- Make a rough sketch and write a brief note in each square to plan what will be on each page.
- Study examples of accordion folded books.
- Fold and cut a sheet of copy paper in half to make two long strips.
- Double the length by taping or gluing the two strips together.
- Fold the strip in half, then in half again twice more.
- Bend every other fold back to make an accordion.
- Use your book map to sketch each page in pencil.
- Finish the art in your book with a black pen or colored pencils.
- Design a cover.
- Fold the book flat and tie it closed with a piece of yarn, string, or ribbon.

Extensions:

- Find out what flight engineers have learned from dragonflies. Plan or create a display showing why dragonfly flight is amazing.
- Create a quiz titled "Ten Weird Facts About Dragonflies."
- Online or in the library, find several haiku poems about insects. Write your own haiku about a dragonfly.

Resources for Teachers:

14 Fun Facts About Dragonflies
    https://www.smithsonianmag.com/science-nature/14-fun-facts-about-dragonflies-96882693/
Introduction to the Odonata: Dragonflies and Damselflies
    http://www.ucmp.berkeley.edu/arthropoda/uniramia/odonatoida.html
Methods: Accordion Books
    https://centerforbookarts.org/methods-accordion-books/
The Secret of Dragonflies' Flight
    https://phys.org/news/2014-11-secret-dragonflies-flight.html
Nature Haiku
    https://www.poets.org/nature-haiku

STEAM Skills:

Science: animal science, life sciences, insects, life cycles
Technology: using the Internet for research
Engineering: researching flight engineering
Arts: bookbinding, scientific illustration, writing poetry

Dog Breeding: Heredity in Action

Objective: To learn how characteristics are passed on to offspring due to selective breeding.

Materials:

Internet access   Scissors   Glue stick   Markers   Large sheet of paper

Student Procedure:

- Choose two AKC (American Kennel Club) dog breeds. Print and cut out a picture of each.
- Create two columns on the paper. Glue one of the dog pictures at the top of each column.
- Under each picture, list the breed's characteristics. Include temperament as well as size, long or short hair, tail type, ears, and snout.
- Combine the two breeds to make a hybrid or "designer" dog breed. Combine the names of the two AKC breeds to name your new breed.
- Predict what your dog will look like and what its temperament will be like. Write a brief paragraph detailing your prediction.
- Search the Internet for a picture of a hybrid dog matching your mix. Print out a picture. If you cannot find an example of your mix, draw a picture of what you think it will look like.

Extensions:

- Create a slide show or display tracing the development of modern horses, cattle, pigs, cats, or other animals from ancient or wild ancestors.
- Model or sketch a section of DNA. Write a short explanation of the role of DNA to go with your model or sketch.
- Make a graph showing how much DNA other animals share with humans. Include, at least, dogs, mice, chickens, and pigs. Write a short explanation of why shared DNA is important for human medical research and treatments.

Resources for Teachers:

Artificially Selecting Dogs
  http://www.ucmp.berkeley.edu/education/lessons/breeding_dogs/
Life Science—Genetics & Selective Breeding
  https://mnliteracy.org/sites/default/files/curriculum/unit_4.7_genetics__selective_breeding.pdf
America's Oldest Dog Discovery Helps Solve Canine DNA Riddle
  https://www.nationalgeographic.com/science/2018/07/news-ancient-dog-breed-dna-koster-ctvt/
Village Dog DNA Reveals Genetic Changes Caused by Domestication
  https://blogs.biomedcentral.com/on-biology/2018/06/28/village-dog-dna-reveals-genetic-changes-caused-by-domestication/
Ancient Wolf DNA Could Solve Dog Origin Mystery
  https://www.livescience.com/50928-wolf-genome-dog-ancient-ancestor.html

STEAM Skills:

Science: animal science, heredity, genetics, DNA
Technology: Internet research, presentation software
Engineering: researching animal breeding
Arts: scientific illustration, making a model
Mathematics: graphing

Observe Animal Heads: Design a Critter Mask

Objective: To carefully observe characteristics of an animal head.

Materials:
Paper
Pencils
Reference photographs
(For extension: photos of sample masks, construction paper, scissors, ruler, glue)

Student Procedure:

- Select an animal to study.
- Find as many photographs of the animal's head as possible.
- Notice the location of the eyes, the shape of the nose or snout, the kinds of teeth, and the placement of the ears.
- Sketch the head from the front, side, and back.
- Which feature makes the animal most recognizable? Why is that feature important to the animal's survival?
- Study pictures of paper animal masks.
- Decide if you want to create a mask that is life size or one that is bigger or smaller to scale.
- Visit a site that explains the basics of paper engineering.
- Design, cut, and fold ears for your animal.
- Using scrap paper, experiment with cutting out eyes like those of your animal.
- Make sketches of possible masks based on your animal's features. Label cuts and folds.

Extensions:
- Use your plans to create a cut-and-folded paper mask.
- Use your reference materials and sketches to create an animal head using natural or craft clay.
- Examine a pop-up book. Design and create a pop-up version of your animal's head.

Resources for Teachers:
Design Your Own Animal Masks
    https://www.kingsnews.org/articles/design-your-own-animal-masks
Family Activity: Fantastic Animal Masks
    http://archive.artic.edu/african/resource/1036
Fold These Amazing Geometric Animal Masks from Cardstock
    https://makezine.com/2015/10/14/amazing-geometric-animal-masks/
Origami Animal Mask
    https://tag.wonderhowto.com/origami-animal-mask/

STEAM Skills:
Science: animal science, animal senses, adaptations, camouflage
Technology: Internet research
Engineering: paper folding, designing a mask
Arts: mask making, origami, sketching
Mathematics: measurement, scale

Bird Beak and Food Match: Design a Card Deck

Objective: To research the relationship between the form and function of bird beaks.

Materials:
    Index cards
    Markers
    Internet access or reference books about birds

Student Procedure:

- Choose a sandpiper, a parrot, a hawk, a duck, a pelican, a robin, a heron, a crane, an eagle, a vulture (or ten other birds with interesting beaks)
- Find out what each bird eats.
- Make 10 cards with pictures of the birds' beaks. Under the picture, write the name of the bird and a phrase to describe the function of the beak, such as "to crush seeds."
- Then make 10 cards with pictures of each bird's favorite food.
- Combine your deck with two other friends.
- Play Bird Beak War.

Extensions:
- Design an imaginary bird for a movie about a paradise planet. The bird eats bugs that live in the sand near the shore of a large shallow lake. Its enemies are large furry creatures that hunt at night. Draw a diagram of your creature. Explain how its beak, wings, and legs help it survive.
- Write a children's story about how the bird in your picture first learned to use its beak or how its beak saved it.

Resources for Teachers:
Bird Beaks
   http://www.fernbank.edu/Birding/bird_beaks.htm
Adaptations: Sipping
   http://projectbeak.org/adaptations/beaks_sipping.htm
Beaks!
   http://www.birdsleuth.org/beaks/
Bird Beaks
   http://www.backyardnature.net/birdbeak.htm

STEAM Skills:
Science: animal science, ornithology, adaptations
Technology: using the Internet for research
Engineering: designing imaginary bird
Arts: scientific illustration, imaginative creature drawing, writing fiction for a specific audience

Tracks and Scat: Create Reference Cards for Nature Hikes

Objective: To identify local animals through observable evidence.

Materials:
 Index cards
 Access to the Internet, a large library, or a local nature center
 Colored markers or colored pencils

Student Procedure:
- List wild and domestic land animals that live in your region. (Include reptiles, amphibians, and birds, as well as mammals.)
- Make a card for each animal. Print its name on the front. Turn the card over. Print "Tracks" at the top and "Scat" at the bottom. Design your cards so they are attractive and easy to read.
- Use an available resource, such as the Internet, to find a photograph of each animal.
- Then find a picture of each creature's track and a picture or description of its scat.
- Use your reference photographs to draw a picture of each animal on the front of its card. Then draw its tracks and scat on the back.
- Create an introductory card for your deck explaining how tracks and scat can reveal information about animals.

Extensions:
- Use plaster of paris to make a casting of an animal track.
- Wearing a mask and gloves, use a stick to examine scat in the field. Record your observations.
- Choose one animal. Find out how many individuals live in your neighborhood, city, county, or region. Use a chart or graph to show whether that number is rising or falling over a period of years or decades.

Resources for Teachers:
Scat & Droppings Identification Key
 http://icwdm.org/Inspection/Scat1.aspx
Scat and Pellets
 http://www.biokids.umich.edu/guides/tracks_and_sign/leavebehind/scat/
What Animal is It?
 https://www.mspca.org/animal_protection/what-animal-is-it/
Living with Wildlife in Illinois
 https://extension.illinois.edu/wildlife/identify_scat.cfm

STEAM Skills:
Science: animal science, scat, ecology
Technology: using the Internet for research
Arts: scientific illustration, design, color, lettering, casting
Mathematics: graphing, statistics

How Not to Be Seen: Fascinating Animal Camouflage

Objective: To research defensive color patterns and use the information to create camouflage for an imaginary animal.

Materials:

Internet access
Paper, pencil, colored pencils or crayons

Student Procedure:

- Conduct an Internet search to find different kinds of animal camouflage.
- Draw a fantasy animal. (Combine elements of two or three real animals or work directly from your imagination.)
- Add your animal's habitat to the drawing.
- Design a camouflage pattern that will help your animal hide from predators.
- Add the design to your animal.

Extensions:

- Investigate the types of coloring scientists think dinosaurs had. Explain why they think so. What proof have they uncovered?
- Design a camouflage design for a desert warrior, a rainforest dweller, or a conifer forest game hunter.
- Create a camouflage design for the environment around your school or home.
- Study some of Bev Doolittle's camouflage paintings. Do a drawing or painting in this style.

Resources for Teachers:

Camouflage
   https://www.nationalgeographic.org/encyclopedia/camouflage/
How Common Animals Use Camouflage to Their Benefit
   https://www.thoughtco.com/camouflage-129662
Discreet by Design: How Hyperstealth's Algorithms Build Better Camo
   https://www.wired.com/2012/06/how-hyperstealths-algorithms-build-better-camo/
This Dinosaur Wore Camouflage
   https://news.nationalgeographic.com/2016/09/dinosaur-camouflage-fossil-find/
Lost in the Wilderness
   https://slate.com/technology/2012/07/camouflage-problems-in-the-army-the-ucp-and-the-future-of-digital-camo.html
Bev Doolittle's "Hide and Seek Cameo D"
   https://www.artifactsgallery.com/art.asp?!=W&ID=13272

STEAM Skills:

Science: animal science, adaptations, defenses, paleontology
Technology: using computer for Internet research
Engineering: designing effective camouflage for hunting and military use
Arts: textile design, abstraction, painting

Local Lives: A Backyard or Campus Habitat Documentary

Objective: To research local habitats and document them.

Materials:

Small notebook and pencil
Video camera or phone capable of creating videos
Computer with video production software

Student Procedure:

- Take a walk around the neighborhood or school campus.
- Make notes about the kinds of trees and plants you see. Add any mammals, reptiles, or insects you see or have seen in the area in the past. Share information with your companions.
- Visit a site online with natural history information about your area. Add facts and details to your notes.
- Visit the following site or another site about how to make a storyboard.

    How to Make a Storyboard for Video
        https://photography.tutsplus.com/tutorials/how-to-make-a-storyboard-for-video--cms-26374

- Use your notes to create a storyboard for a video documentary about your area.
- Write a script for your narrator to read.

Extensions:

- Film your documentary. Use video production software to edit the film and add narration. Public domain music is available online. If you play an instrument, record your own theme.
- Create a movie poster for your documentary.
- Stage a film festival sharing several documentaries from your class or group.
- Plan and/or construct a wildlife garden for your campus. Include labeled plants and an Internet guide for visitors.
- Write a fantasy story set in your backyard or on your campus.

Resources for Teachers:

17 Tips for Making Your Backyard Wildlife Friendly on a Budget
    https://www.audubon.org/news/17-tips-making-your-backyard-wildlife-friendly-budget
Backyard Animals
    http://www.backyardnature.net/animals.htm
Backyard Science: Tallying Local Species to Learn About Diversity
    https://learning.blogs.nytimes.com/2012/05/02/backyard-science-tallying-local-species-to-learn-about-diversity/

STEAM Skills:

Science: animal and plant sciences, ecology, biomes
Technology: using computers, video equipment, and video production software
Engineering: landscape design, garden construction
Arts: videography, landscape design, music, storyboards, writing narration
Mathematics: measurement and scale for garden

Arrival on Planet X: Develop a Science Fiction Habitat

Objective: To use understanding of ecosystems to create a believable fictional world.

Materials:
   Paper and pencil or computer and word-processing software
   Crayons, colored pencils, or markers

Student Procedure:
- Draw a picture of a landscape on Earth-like Planet X. Label herbivores and carnivores. Show plants flowering, spreading seeds, growing, and decomposing. Invent large and small animals. Invent names and label them.
- Write an account of your arrival on the planet, describing what you see, hear, feel, and smell. Include air temperature and water sources.

Extensions:
- Write a story or make a (very) short graphic novel about a space explorer's adventure on Planet X.
- Watch a favorite film about another planet. Write a short review explaining why the world in the film is believable or why it isn't.
- Imagine you are a thumb-sized alien who has landed in a town park near you. Describe the park from the alien's point of view.

Resources for Teachers:
   Planets in Science Fiction
      https://en.wikipedia.org/wiki/Planets_in_science_fiction
   Sci-Fi's Coolest Worlds
      https://www.ign.com/articles/2009/10/14/sci-fis-coolest-worlds
   What is an Extremophile?
      https://oceanservice.noaa.gov/facts/extremophile.html
   Life—But Not as We Know It
      https://www.chemistryworld.com/features/life-on-other-planets/3008503.article

STEAM Skills:
   Science: animal and plant sciences, biomes, life science
   Technology: using word-processing software
   Engineering: designing an alien world
   Arts: creative writing, science fiction, imaginative illustration, graphic novel illustration
   Mathematics: scale measurements

Monster on the Loose: A Newscast

Objective: To use knowledge of animal traits to describe a believable monster.

Materials:

Voice or video recording device

Paper and pencil or computer and word-processing software

A sample radio or TV newscast

Student Procedure:

- Listen to or watch a segment of a radio or television news broadcast.
- Note the elements of the announcement such as the "hook" to catch interest, people or places involved, and any expert opinions cited.
- List the characteristics of your favorite monster from books, TV, or films. What characteristics does it share with actual living things? How does it differ?
- Using your observations, create a believable new monster. Make notes describing it in detail, including characteristics that would make it a threat to humans.
- Write a script for a radio news broadcast warning listeners that your monster is about to attack the city. Use details from your notes to make the announcement convincing.

Extensions:

- Record or videotape your broadcast. Share it with another group.
- Draw, paint, or create a model of your monster.
- Devise a way your monster could be destroyed. Before doing this, be ready to explain your creature's requirements for life.
- Write a story about a human hero's encounter with your monster.

Resources for Teachers:

The War of the Worlds (Radio Drama)
https://en.wikipedia.org/wiki/The_War_of_the_Worlds_(radio_drama)

Index of Fictional Creatures
https://tvtropes.org/pmwiki/pmwiki.php/Main/IndexOfFictionalCreatures

Creatures and Monsters from Greek Mythology
https://greekgodsandgoddesses.net/creatures/

Greek Monsters
https://www.nationalgeographic.org/media/greek-monsters/

What Preys on Humans?
https://www.smithsonianmag.com/science-nature/what-preys-on-humans-34332952/

Writing Monsters: What Makes a Monster Scary?
https://www.writersdigest.com/online-editor/writing-monsters-scary-qualities

STEAM Skills:

Science: animal science, predators, defenses

Technology: using audio and/or video recording devices and software, using word-processing software

Engineering: designing a model

Arts: writing science fiction, script writing, audio or video performance, drawing or painting imaginary creatures

Once Endangered—Still Endangered: Science-Based Poetry

Objective: To write and present a poem about endangered animals based on research.

Materials:

Paper and pencil or computer and word-processing software
Colored pencils
Internet connection or current reference texts about endangered species

Student Procedure:

- Use online or other sources to find an animal that is extinct or that is endangered but has been saved from extinction.
- Note why the creature was endangered and what happened to tip the balance toward or away from extinction.
- Write a poem using facts from your notes. It does not have to rhyme, but it should use poetic elements such as rhythm, repetition, alliteration, and figurative speech.
- The first half of the poem should show why the animal was in danger and the second half should demonstrate how it was saved. If it is extinct, tell about any efforts that were made to save it.
- Poems, like films, draw their power from emotions. Aim to make your audience feel regret or relief about the outcome.

Extensions:

- Design a pamphlet for Earth Day showing past successes credited, in part, to the event.
- Write an editorial for the school or local newspaper explaining why your favorite endangered species should be protected. Include steps people or the government should take to save these creatures.
- Draw or make a model of an extinct animal. Write a description to accompany it. Include when and where it lived, along with the reason for its extinction.
- Make a graph showing estimated numbers of endangered animals 50 years ago, ten years ago, and today.
- Hold a poetry reading for Earth Day. Share the poems written by your group or class.

Resources for Teachers:

Species Directory
  https://www.worldwildlife.org/species/directory?sort=extinction_status&direction=desc
Poetic Forms
  https://www.poets.org/poetsorg/collection/poetic-forms
48 Environmental Victories Since the First Earth Day
  https://news.nationalgeographic.com/2016/04/160422-earth-day-46-facts-environment/

STEAM Skills:

Science: animal science, ecology, endangered animals, conservation
Technology: using word-processing software
Engineering: designing a model
Arts: writing and performing poetry, graphic design, drawing
Mathematics: graphing

I Lived in This Shell: A Mollusk Monologue

Objective: To write a dramatic monologue using research about mollusks.

Materials:

Paper and pencil or computer and word-processing software
Access to the Internet or reference materials about mollusks
Mollusk shells
Video camera or phone (optional)
Online or other research materials about the life cycles of mollusks.

Student Procedure:

- Choose a mollusk shell.
- Use online or text resources to identify the creature that once lived in it. Find out where this mollusk probably lived, how it came into the world, what it ate, and who its enemies were.
- Use the information you have discovered to write a first-person narrative from the point of view of your mollusk.
- Imagining that you are the creature, write about your days in the sea. Include things you enjoyed most and things you feared.
- Make your acting debut. Present your monologue to the group. Use what you have learned about your creature to present its story convincingly.

Extensions:

- Videotape your group's monologues.
- Create a storyboard for a picture book about a mollusk's life.
- Make a shell collection, identifying each mollusk with a label.
- Create a display showing why mollusks are important to humans.

Resources for Teachers:

Types of Mollusks
   https://www.ck12.org/book/CK-12-Life-Science-Concepts-For-Middle-School/section/9.8/
Molluscs: Phylum Mollusca
   http://www.biologyeducation.net/natural-history/molluscs/
The Phylum Mollusca
   https://www.earthlife.net/inverts/mollusca.html

STEAM Skills:

Science: animal science, oceanography
Technology: using video devices and software, using word-processing software, using online resources to research and identify mollusks
Engineering: designing a display and identification system for mollusks
Arts: creative writing, dramatic arts, acting, storyboard design and drawing

Squishy Squirty Squid: Dissection

Objective: To learn about squid anatomy through actual or virtual dissection.

Materials:

A bag of small fresh or freshly defrosted squid (fish market or Asian market)
Plastic gloves   Scissors or dissecting knives
Tweezers   Paper plates
Newspapers for covering tables   Paper, pencils, and colored pencils
Charts of external and internal squid anatomy (from online or text sources)

Student Procedure:

- Examine the external features of the squid. Count the arms. The two longer ones are called tentacles. Draw a detailed sketch of one. Include the suction cups. Notice how the tentacles are different from the arms.
- Locate the fins, the eyes, and the mantle. Notice the spots. They help the squid change color.
- Open out the arms and find the squid's mouth parts, called the beak.
- Locate the siphon. Lay the squid on the plate with its siphon facing up.
- With scissors, cut the mantle to expose the internal organs.
- Locate the ink sac, the gills, the cecum, and the hearts. You also may be able to find the liver, brain, and nidamental gland.
- Make a sketch of the squid showing the location of all the body parts you found.

Extensions:

- Videotape or photograph the dissection procedure. Write and record a script explaining each step. Share this documentary with another group.
- Make a display showing why squid are important in a marine ecosystem.
- Paint an underwater landscape showing squid in their natural habitat. Include other creatures that share the same biome.

Resources for Teachers:

Dissection: Don't Cut Out Safety
     https://www.nsta.org/publications/news/story.aspx?id=53340
Facts About Squids
     https://www.squid-world.com/
The Squid Biologist Connecting Schools and Scientists Worldwide
     https://www.nature.com/articles/d41586-018-06772-9
Squid Dissection
     http://njseagrant.org/wp-content/uploads/2014/03/squid_dissection.pdf
The Id of Squid
     https://www.coastalliving.com/food/seafood-basics/id-squid

STEAM Skills:

Science: animal science, oceanography, dissection, observation
Technology: using video equipment or camera, video presentation device and software
Arts: scientific illustration, videography/photography, script writing
Mathematics: possible measurement and use of scale when examining and drawing the squid

Exercise and Pulse Rate: Graphing the Beat

Objective: To observe and quantify the effects of activity on pulse rate.

Materials:
Stopwatch (or a clock with a second hand)
Lined paper and pencils
Graph paper and colored pencils (Or online graphing software)

Student Procedure:
- Choose a partner.
- Both partners create charts with three columns and two rows. Label the first row Subject A and the second row Subject B. Label the columns Resting, Mild, and Strenuous.
- One participant, Subject A, places two fingers on his or her radial artery (on inside of the wrist near the thumb) and counts the beats.
- The other tells the subject when 15 seconds has passed.
- Both participants multiply the number of beats by four (since 4 x 15 = 60 seconds) and record the result in the first column. This is the beats per minute while resting.
- Partners trade places. The timer becomes Subject B and Subject A keeps the time.
- Repeat the procedure after mild exercise (walking in place for one minute).
- Repeat it again after one minute of strenuous exercise (jumping in place for one minute).
- Record each set of statistics in the proper column and row.
- Use the statistics gathered to design a graph that will help others understand the results. Each participant should create a different kind of graph.

Extensions:
- Draw or build a model of the human heart. Explain why blood pulses through the arteries instead of flowing at a constant pace.
- Draw a chart showing the human circulatory system. Include the major veins and arteries. Explain why illustrators usually use red to depict arteries and blue to depict veins.
- Compile the group's results into a single graph.

Resources for Teachers:
Marathon Challenge
  https://www.pbs.org/wgbh/nova/education/activities/3414_marathon.html
Sweaty Science: How Does Heart Rate Change with Exercise?
  https://www.scientificamerican.com/article/bring-science-home-heart-rate-excercise/
How Wearable Heart-rate Monitors Work, and Which is Best for You
  https://arstechnica.com/gadgets/2017/04/how-wearable-heart-rate-monitors-work-and-which-is-best-for-you/

STEAM Skills:
Science: human body, physiology, circulatory system, the heart
Technology: using a stopwatch
Engineering: designing a model
Art: scientific illustration, model building
Mathematics: timing, statistics, sampling and extrapolating, graphing

Sweet Saltines: Digestion Begins in the Mouth

Objective: To observe the role of enzymes in digestion.

Materials:

Unsalted saltine crackers   White bread (for extension)

Digital timer or stopwatch   Internet connection or texts about digestion

NOTE: Make sure students are not allergic or sensitive to any ingredients in the cracker or bread before proceeding.

Student Procedure:

- Put a cracker in your mouth and chew it.
- Write a short description of the texture (the way the cracker felt in your mouth) and the taste.
- Set the timer for 90 seconds or 1.5 minutes. Put another cracker in your mouth, but do not chew it for 90 seconds. When the time is up, chew the cracker and swallow.
- Write a short description of the texture and the taste.
- In your digestive system, substances called enzymes change food into a form your cells can use for fuel. The change in taste gives you a clue about cell food. What is it?
- Use the Internet or texts to find the name of the enzyme in saliva that starts the digestive process.
- Use your notes to write a short essay describing the entire experiment, present the information in comic strip form, or create a slide presentation.

Extensions:

- Repeat the experiment with small pieces of a slice of bread. Notice the similarities or differences.
- Draw a diagram of the human digestive system. Label it with the enzymes found in each location.
- Explain the role physical grinding and mashing play in different parts of the digestive tract. Create a display or slide show to demonstrate where these strong-arm tactics are used.
- Create a recipe collection featuring mechanical or chemical processes that make foods easier for the body to use. (Tenderizing is one example.)

Resources for Teachers:

The Digestive System
    https://www.stem.org.uk/resources/elibrary/resource/36133/digestive-system

Digestive System
    https://www.nationalgeographic.com/science/health-and-human-body/human-body/digestive-system/

Enzymes Lesson Plans
    https://www.ngsslifescience.com/science.php?/biology/lessonplans/C400/

Enzymes Science Fair Projects
    http://www.all-science-fair-projects.com/category105.html

STEAM Skills:

Science: human body, biology, enzymes, digestive system

Technology: using stopwatch or digital timer, using slide show presentation software

Art: scientific illustration, culinary arts, nonfiction writing (personal experience), comic strip illustration

Fingerprints: Leaving Your Mark

Objective: To examine and compare fingerprints.

Materials:

Cocoa powder (Note: ink pads can be used instead)
Small plate or piece of foil
Paper towels or baby wipes for cleaning hands
Internet connection or texts

Paper
Magnifiers

Student Procedure:

- Pour a little cocoa powder on the plate or foil.
- Press the pad of your index finger in the powder.
- Press the finger on the paper.
- Examine the print with the magnifier.
- Online or in a text, find examples of basic fingerprint ridge patterns. They include various types of arches, loops, and whorls.
- List the ones you find in your fingerprint.
- Repeat the procedure with other fingers on the same hand or on your other hand.
- Compare prints with a partner.

Extensions:

- Create a display showing the features of fingerprints or the uses of fingerprinting in forensics.
- Use ink or paint to create an artwork composed of individual fingerprints.
- Use a cell phone or digital camera to photograph your fingerprint and enlarge it. Create a slide presentation pointing out the ridge patterns and characteristics in your print.
- Create a slide presentation about the history of fingerprinting or forensic sciences.

Resources for Teachers:

What Type of Fingerprint Are You?
  https://www.nsta.org/sciencematters/docs/Shippensburg-FingerPrinting2.pdf
Forensics Fingerprinting Lesson Grades 9-12
  https://www.oercommons.org/authoring/9440-forensics-fingerprinting-lesson-grades-9-12/view
Patterns and Fingerprints
  https://www.teachengineering.org/activities/view/cub_spect_activity1
Fingerprint Evidence
  https://www.sciencenewsforstudents.org/article/fingerprint-evidence
She's a dab hand at this! Artist uses just her fingerprints to create huge murals with charcoal
  https://www.dailymail.co.uk/news/article-2234831/Judith-Ann-Braun-Artist-uses-just-fingerprints-create-huge-murals-charcoal.html

STEAM Skills:

Science: human body, forensic science, natural variability
Technology: using magnification tools, using a camera, using slide presentation software
Arts: printing, composition, texture, unconventional tools

From the Sun to the Kuiper Belt: A Campus Scale Model

Objective: To design a model depicting distances in the solar system to scale.

Materials:
Internet connection   Calculators or computers
A scale map of the school campus (metric, if possible)
Optional: Sidewalk chalk   String or rope   Rolling measuring device or measuring tapes

Student Procedure:
- Use a text or the Internet to find the distance between the sun and each planet using the metric scale or Astronomical Units (AU). (NASA offers a great resource at "How Big is Our Solar System" https://www.nasa.gov/sites/default/files/files/YOSS_Act1.pdf.)
- Consult the campus map. Locate the best possible location for your model. This will be a long straight section such as a fenceline.
- Select the longest even length. For example, if the edge of your campus is 15.8 meters long, make the orbit of the most distant planet 10 meters from your sun. (If the measurements on your campus map are not metric, convert them using a formula and calculator or an online coversion chart.)
- Use what you know about proportions. Write an equation to find the distance, in meters, between the location of your sun on one end of the fenceline and Neptune on the other. Using similar equations, find scale distances to the rest of the planets.
- (If you want to check your numbers or create miniature planets, use this handy calculator from Exploratorium. http://www.exploratorium.edu/ronh/solar_system/)

Extensions:
- Design or create markers for a permanent solar system walk in a local park. Send your proposal to the city council or your town's newspaper. Include a scale map of your proposed site and a budget.
- Create a scale model of the solar system as a science fair project.
- Use a narrow roll of paper such as toilet paper or adding-machine tape to create a scale drawing of the solar system. Display it in a hallway or around a classroom (near the ceiling.)

Resources for Teachers:
Watch This Guy Build a Massive Solar System in the Desert
   https://www.youtube.com/watch?v=Kj4524AAZdE
Solar System Model   http://thinkzone.wlonk.com/SS/SolarSystemModel.php
The Thousand-Yard Model or, The Earth as a Peppercorn
   https://www.noao.edu/education/peppercorn/pcmain.html
Voyage Scale Model Solar System
   https://www.jeffreybennett.com/model-solar-systems/voyage-scale-model-solar-system/

STEAM Skills:
Science: space science, solar system, distances in space
Technology: computer skills, Internet research, using calculator
Engineering: designing scale model
Arts: scientific illustration, model building
Mathematics: metric conversions, large numbers, proportions, scale models, ratios, budgets

The Life of a Star: A Slide Show

Objective: To research the life cycles of stars and share results in an interesting and understandable way.

Materials:

Paper and pencil   Markers
Internet access   Slide presentation software

Student Procedure:
- Use the keywords "life of a star" to perform an Internet search.
- List the stages in a large, medium, or small star's growth, development, and demise.
- Create a storyboard to plan your presentation's slides.
- Visit the NASA site to locate images for your presentation. (They are all public domain.)
  https://www.nasa.gov/multimedia/imagegallery/index.html
- Write a script to accompany your presentation. Many programs will allow you to record narration.
- Create your presentation.

Extensions:
- Share your presentation online, with another class, or as part of a science fair project.
- Paint a picture of what you think the formation of a supernova or black hole looks like. You can use watercolors or tempera paints or try techniques such as splatter painting or paint pouring with acrylic paints.
- Write a story about what the residents of a planet do when they learn that there sun is declining. Do they try to fix the sun, move to a new solar system, or come up with some other solution?

Resources for Teachers:
Life Cycle of a Star
  https://www.schoolsobservatory.org/learn/astro/stars/cycle
The Life Cycles of Stars: How Supernovae Are Formed
  https://imagine.gsfc.nasa.gov/educators/lessons/xray_spectra/background-lifecycles.html
What Is a Supernova?
  https://www.space.com/6638-supernova.html
How to Make an Element
  https://www.pbs.org/wgbh/nova/article/make-an-element/
How to Splatter Paint
  https://www.wikihow.com/Splatter-Paint
How to Do a Pour Painting: A Tutorial for Beginners
  https://feltmagnet.com/painting/How-to-Do-a-Pour-Painting

STEAM Skills:
Science: space science, astronomy, stars, cycles
Technology: using slide presentation software, Internet research, computers
Arts: presentation design, script writing, painting, creative writing
Mathematics: large numbers, metric system, exponents, charts

Lunar and Solar Eclipses: Flashlight Investigations

Objective: To demonstrate lunar and solar eclipses.

Materials:
Flashlight or electric lantern   Beach ball   Tennis ball

Student Procedure:
- Work in groups of three. One student will hold the flashlight. Another will be the Earth and hold the beach ball. The third will be the moon and hold the tennis ball.
- Watch an online video demonstrating a lunar eclipse or read about lunar eclipses in a text.
- Turn off the lights in the room. Turn on the flashlight or lantern. Work with members of your group to demonstrate how a lunar eclipse occurs.
- Repeat the process to demonstrate a solar eclipse. (Hint, this is harder.)

Extensions:
- Create a video of your group's demonstration.
- Create a chart showing the dates of the next three lunar eclipses visible in your area.
- Create a slide presentation showing how a solar eclipse occurs. Include stories people have told about solar eclipses in the past.
- Paint a landscape on Earth or another planet with a total solar eclipse.
- Pretend you don't know what causes eclipses. Write an original story explaining why the sun disappears and reappears. Your tale could involve monsters or something else. Add illustrations to create a picture book, or dim the lights and tell your story to the group. Make your friends laugh, scream, or gasp.

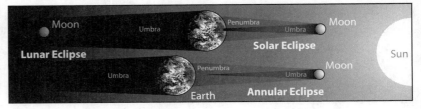

Resources for Teachers:
NASA Eclipse Website
   https://eclipse.gsfc.nasa.gov/eclipse.html
Modeling a Solar Eclipse
   https://airandspace.si.edu/sites/default/files/iss-eclipse.pdf
Earth's Eclipses Are Special
   https://earthsky.org/earth/eclipses-on-earth-and-other-planets
How Artists Have Depicted Eclipses Across History
   https://www.theatlantic.com/science/archive/2016/09/an-artists-view-of-an-eclipse/498548/
Epic Eclipse: A 'Pi in the Sky' Math Challenge
   https://www.jpl.nasa.gov/edu/teach/activity/epic-eclipse-a-pi-in-the-sky-challenge/

STEAM Skills:
Science: space science, astronomy, eclipses
Technology: Internet research, using video equipment and presentation software
Arts: writing fiction, point of view, illustration, storytelling
Mathematics: measurement, charts and graphs

Our Solar System's Planets: Planning Scale Models

Objective: To plan and construct scale models of the planets.

Materials:
Paper
Pencils
Computers
Internet access

Student Procedure:
- Use a recent text or the Internet to find the diameter of each actual planet.
- Choose a diameter in inches or centimeters for the largest model. (Consider the size of the table where you will display your finished planets. If Jupiter is more than 10 inches, they won't fit.)
- Use what you know about proportions. Write equations to determine the diameter of each model planet.
- Use a compass and ruler to create a scale drawing of each model planet. Determine the correct color by consulting photos online or in a text.

Extensions:
- Use craft books or online sources to develop a technique for modeling planets. Ideas include papier mache and craft clay. Model one of the planets and its moons.
- Create a slide presentation about your favorite planet or our star, the sun. Include how it differs from other members of the solar system, the length of its day and year, its atmosphere, and what we know about its surface.
- Create a picture book about the planets. Use words preschoolers will understand. Compare the sizes of the planets to familiar things such as raisins, watermelons, or apples. Make your proportions as accurate as possible. (Warning: This may be very difficult.)

Resources for Teachers:
The Planets in Our Solar System in Order of Size
    https://www.universetoday.com/36649/planets-in-order-of-size/
Scale Model of the Solar System
    https://www.education.com/science-fair/article/scale-model-planets-solar-system/
Sizes and Distances
    https://www.kean.edu/~fosborne/resources/ex11c2.htm
Planetary Size and Distance Comparison
    https://www.nationalgeographic.org/activity/planetary-size-and-distance-comparison/

STEAM Skills:
Science: space science, astronomy, solar system, planets
Technology: Internet research, using presentation software
Engineering: designing planet models
Arts: illustration, model making, papier mache or clay sculpture, nonfiction writing
Mathematics: large numbers, astronomical units (AU), measurement, metric system, scale, proportions, geometry, circles, diameter

Designing and Testing a Human Sundial

Objective: To observe the rotation of the Earth.

Materials:

    Battery-operated analog clock   Rope

    Sidewalk chalk   A paved surface

    A sunny day

Student Procedure:

- On a paved section of the campus, use a 6- to 10-foot length of rope and a piece of sidewalk chalk to draw a circle. (One student stands still while another, keeping the rope taut, walks around, drawing a line.)
- The student in the center is the style. If the day is sunny, the student's body will cast a shadow on the pavement.
- Lay the clock on the ground so the hour hand is pointing the same direction and is at the same angle as the shadow.
- Use chalk to draw a circle around the feet of the student acting as the style.
- On the chalk circle, mark the spot across from the shadow. In large numbers, write the hour. For example, if the clock reads 11:10, mark that spot on the circle 11.
- Keep the clock flat on the ground. Don't move it. The hour hand should line up with the mark on the circle and the direction of the shadow. Use it to help you fill in the other hour marks.
- Stand in the middle of the circle and check the time later in the day. Does it work? Why or why not?

Extensions:

- Check the time the next week or the next month. Keep track of how much the dial's accuracy changes. Use texts or the Internet to find out why.
- Design a human sundial installation or a sundial sculpture for your yard or a park. Use online or text sources to help you make it accurate and durable. Locate the materials you need in catalogs and estimate the cost of your project. Propose it to your local parks department or your parents.

Resources for Teachers:

Making a Sundial

    http://lasp.colorado.edu/home/wp-content/uploads/2011/08/sundial.pdf

Changing Shadows

    https://www.nasa.gov/topics/solarsystem/sunearthsystem/main/PO_makeAndTake.html

Portable Sundial

    https://www.teachengineering.org/activities/view/portable_sundial

STEAM Skills:

Science: space and atmospheric science, solar system, Earth's rotation, time

Technology: time measurement with analog clock and sundial, Internet research

Engineering: sundial design

Arts: functional sculpture

Mathematics: geometry, circle construction, arcs, angles